How to win

A guide to successful
community campaigning

FRIENDS *of the*
earth
for the planet for people

Editors: Elaine Gilligan and Anna Watson

Thanks to the following people for their help with writing this book:
Tricia Allen, Nicola Baird, Hazel Barnes, Debbie Bell, Mike Birkin, David
Bloy, Tony Bosworth, Vanessa Carey, Anne Chapman, Mike Childs, Chris
Crean, John Dunckley, Lisa Fagan, Paul Fitzgerald, Elli Groner, Brenda
Lardner, Chas Linn, Rita Marcangelo, Paul Mason, Julian Mellor, Viv
Mountford, Andy Neather, Donald Ritchie, Ben Rogers, Julian Rosser, Joe
Short, Lesley Smeardon, Liana Stupples, Mary Taylor, Deb Thompson,
Joanna Watson, Martyn Williams, Ian Willmore, Paul de Zylva

Cartoons: Paul Fitzgerald

ISBN 1 85750 331 7

© Friends of the Earth, 2000

Friends of the Earth works to protect and improve the conditions for life
on Earth, now and for the future.

Friends of the Earth, 26-28 Underwood Street, London N1 7JQ

Tel: 020 7490 1555
Fax: 020 7490 0881

E-mail: info@foe.co.uk
Website: www.foe.co.uk

Contents   Page

Part 5: Getting to grips with the system
An insider's guide

Part 6: Useful tips

Part 7: Useful contacts

Foreword

by Charles Secrett, Executive Director, Friends of the Earth

How To Win shows you how to be a successful campaigner and still lead a normal life! A little bit of time, a good idea or two, a few materials, energy, activity and some like-minded colleagues are all it takes.

Friends of the Earth provides information and inspiring ideas so that people can find out about the state of their world locally, nationally and globally. "Think global act local!" That was our founding motto. Friends of the Earth helps people to get organised and use their influence together as consumers, voters, shareholders, tax payers and constituents to confront, cajole and persuade companies and governments to do the right thing.

As people learn what is happening to the planet, their first response is usually fear – frightened by the enormity of the environmental crisis, and subdued by the power of companies and governments. There is a lot to worry about, from species extinctions and wild habitat destruction, to climate change and the accelerating spread of dangerous synthetic chemicals. But fear paralyses, it doesn't help create an environmentally friendly planet.

When it's clear who is to blame people become angry. But anger is also not enough; angry people have energy, but they do not listen and learn. It is at this point that people become campaigners. For them, hope begins to grow. Fear and anger turn to commitment and determination. People channel their worries, and use that energy positively. They join with neighbours and family, friends and colleagues, to help bring about change for the better. And it works.

I've seen it happen time and time again: mighty, powerful companies and remote officialdom forced to change because people insist on it. Remember Shell and Nigeria? Monsanto and GM crops? The World Trade Organisation challenged at Seattle? Governments and companies are made up of people too. They can be persuaded to see sense, by motivated folk like you and I who know what we are talking about. That's what campaigning is all about.

How To Win is about bringing hope. It describes many ways forward. Use it well.

Introduction

Campaigning. Big word, lots of meanings... At its simplest, campaigning is about getting organised to change something. We have the right to be involved in decisions that change our lives and unless we exercise that right, those in powerful positions can do what they want to with a minimum of public opposition. We want change – whether it is getting a pedestrian crossing near to the local school or tackling local pollution – so people are getting together with other people and making their views known. We have the power to change things – we choose who we vote for, what we put in our shopping basket and who we invest our money with.

How to Win deals with the basics of how to get started and get organised. You've got the power – this book tells you how to use it and how to win. It covers the bare essentials of how to start a campaign and is aimed at any would-be campaigner who has decided they want to do something. It can be read as a step-by-step guide, or can be dipped in and out of depending on the stage your campaign is at. If you want further information there are also plenty of useful contacts and suggested further reading. In addition we have produced a back-up information pack which contains 10 in-depth fact sheets – details on this pack can be found on page 108.

Part 1 deals with the basics – where to start and how to get organised. Campaigns are seldom won by individuals but by people. This chapter tells you how to go about getting that people power. Part 2 builds on the basics. The key to every successful campaign is the need to be clear about what it is you are trying to do and why. Get that right and the rest falls into place. Once you have got the basics of your campaign in place you need to get your message across.

In a busy world where we are bombarded by images, your campaign message has to be heard. Find out ways to get noticed by following the advice in Part 3. Part 4 shows you in more depth how to use the media, explains how to make effective props from basic materials and gives you tips about how to build your campaign profile. This chapter also looks at relatively new campaigning tools such as e-mail and offers advice about how to build a website. The power of such information technology has transformed the potential to make our views known in all corners of the world. It is about finding and sharing information and networking on a global scale – so do not overestimate how difficult it might seem or underestimate how useful and powerful it is.

Finally Part 5 steers you through the complex world of getting to grips with the system – from finding your way around your local council to lobbying your elected representative. This chapter also touches on the complex issues you may need to grapple with at some stage of your campaign. Each of these issues could be the subject of a book in themselves – we have given you the bare bones with plenty of contacts and suggestions for further reading.

Friends of the Earth is an organisation with a network of more than 200 voluntary local groups throughout England, Wales and Northern Ireland. *How to Win* draws on our years of community-based campaigning. There may be no right way to campaign, but there are tried and tested ways based on experience. There are also no guaranteed outcomes, but you may surprise yourself (and your friends and neighbours) and have a lot of fun as well. *How to Win* cannot provide all the answers, but it does provide anyone who wants to get started with the first steps on how to win. Good luck.

Getting started

People, groups and managing them

Part 1

1 First steps to becoming a campaigner

You could become a campaigner any day. It may be that you are flicking through a local newspaper and find yourself worrying about the plans for a new incinerator outlined in one of the articles. Perhaps you will still be in bed, half listening to the local radio station, when your attention is grabbed by a news item on plans to bulldoze a local green space to make way for a new bypass. Or maybe you will be playing with the kids at the local park and overhear parents talking about how bad local air pollution levels have become.

Instead of hoping someone else will sort the problem out, you ask yourself a few questions:

- ⊙ Do I think this is an important issue?
- ⊙ Does this affect me or my home, or the places where my family and/or my friends live?
- ⊙ Will I feel bad if I don't do something about it?
- ⊙ Can I do something about it?

If the answers to these questions are yes, then you've taken the first step to becoming a campaigner: you've decided to do something. For most local campaigns the starting point will be your local council. At this stage you need to know roughly how decisions are made so you can get started. (For more details on how to influence decision makers see Part 5, page 80.)

At a local level we elect councillors. They are usually unpaid people who devote much of their spare time to helping their communities run smoothly. There are regular council meetings which are usually held at your town hall and are open to the public.

Although Government operates on a larger scale, the decisions it makes are made in a similar way. Members of Parliament are elected by us; laws are debated and then passed by the House of Commons and the House of Lords. The role of national government is changing with the establishment of a Scottish Parliament, Welsh Assembly and Northern Ireland Assembly. It is also likely that

Europe will play an increasingly important role in decision-making in the future. (See Useful reading on page 108 for details on how to get more information on these issues.)

If a local or national company is behind the proposal you are concerned about, the key people to influence will be the company's director, board members, staff and shareholders. (See Useful reading on page 108 for more information on how to influence the corporate sector.)

Check it out
Before you go any further the first priority is to check out the facts. Is something really going to happen or is it a rumour? Is it at a stage where a difference can be made?

More often than not, your local council will be your first point of contact and will be listed in your local telephone book. In Northern Ireland local councils have fewer powers, so your starting point may be the Department of the Environment or the Department of Regional Development (see Useful contacts on page 105). Telephone the general switchboard number or the relevant council department. Before you call, prepare a list of questions to ask. For example:

⊙ Is what I have heard about the Mytown bypass correct?

⊙ Who is in charge of this proposal?

⊙ Has there been any public consultation on this?

⊙ Has a final decision been taken, and if not, when will a decision be made?

⊙ Are there any summaries of the consultation/reports available for members of the public?

When you make the call make sure you are put through to the right person. Be persistent, and take a note of their name and job position. It will help to take notes during the phone call, so you can keep an exact record of what the person has said. This could be useful if they break a promise further down the line.

Can you make a difference?
In that first phone call establish what the problem is and what, if anything, can be done about it. The basic rule is that the earlier you get involved, the better the chances are of winning. The proposal may have already been given the go-ahead or public consultation may have taken place. Either way it's harder (though not

impossible) to campaign when the official decision has been taken or where the opportunity for people to make their views known has passed. Bearing this in mind, consider if it's worth starting a campaign on the issue. If you do decide to go ahead with the campaign you need to start planning.

Laying a paper trail

You've made a telephone call and spoken to the official concerned; you now have information on the issue. Follow this up with a letter outlining:

- ⊙ Your understanding of the council's position, eg, "Following our telephone conversation on 10 July, I understand that there are plans for a Mytown bypass...".
- ⊙ Your concerns.
- ⊙ What you want.

Send copies of this letter to influential local people, including your local councillor and/or your local MP, Welsh Assembly Member, Member of Scottish Parliament or Member of the Legislative Assembly in Northern Ireland. At the bottom of the letter to the council make sure you indicate who else you've copied the letter to. Ideally, when you send copies of your letter, include a covering note explaining your concerns and ask for their support. Make sure you keep a copy for your own reference. As the campaign builds up, so will the paperwork. Keep copies of all correspondence throughout the campaign as you may need to refer back to them at a later date.

Gathering the basic facts

The next step is to collect together the basic facts.

- ⊙ Ask your council, or Department of Environment in Northern Ireland, for any documentation on the proposal, eg, for copies of a planning proposal.
- ⊙ Visit your local library and see if they have any information — such as local press clippings — on the proposal.
- ⊙ Visit the site you are campaigning about and find out who uses it at present. What do people in the neighbourhood think about the proposed plans? Do they know about them? Talking to people is how you begin to get people interested in what you are trying to do.

2 Finding people to give you people power

You've now made a start by writing to the relevant official and gathering basic facts, but you can't do it all on your own. Now is the time to get other people interested.

Campaigns are rarely won by individuals; they are won by groups of concerned people. The more people you involve in your campaign and the more tasks which can be shared, the greater your chances are of campaign success.

One of the commonest complaints from campaigners is that there aren't enough people to do everything, which can lead to overwork and stress for a few committed individuals. The most successful campaigns need the backing of as many people as possible to share the work and to show that the campaign has wide support. Getting more people involved in your campaign will:

- ⊙ Give your group greater credibility.
- ⊙ Enable you to get your message across to a greater number of people.
- ⊙ Provide you with a larger pool of people with particular skills or interests.
- ⊙ Give your group a regular income, for example if people pay a small membership fee.

By now you've established the nature of the problem, and have spoken to a few people who want to get involved. To start your group, get together and decide on a plan of action. You will need to:

- ⊙ Clarify your aims.
- ⊙ Decide how much time you can all spare and how often you want to meet.
- ⊙ Decide on a campaign name.
- ⊙ Make a list of people the group can approach to write letters, attend meetings, or make telephone calls.
- ⊙ Write down a list of other contacts who might be useful.

Having established a core group, you now need to let others:

- ⊙ Know you exist.
- ⊙ Know how to find you.
- ⊙ Know a bit about your campaign.

"We exist!" – tell people

Media coverage is by far the best way of letting thousands of people know you exist. Using the advice in Part 4, page 57, put out a press release announcing the launch of your group, with details about your campaign and where and when the campaign group meets.

Think also about other ways to publicise your existence. Set yourself an exercise: how can you make sure that a stranger getting off the bus in your town would walk for no more than 20 minutes without realising that your campaign group exists? This can be a fun exercise to get your group thinking about. Ideas for promoting your group could include:

- ⊙ Advertising meetings in the local press (many papers run a free listings column).
- ⊙ Writing to your local letters pages asking for help with specific events, such as fundraising, or appealing for specific skills.
- ⊙ Giving talks to other organisations and encouraging their members to join.
- ⊙ Putting up eye-catching posters advertising your group's meetings in venues such as shops, libraries, community centres, sports centres and members' front windows.

Campaign publicity should always state:

- ⊙ What your group does.
- ⊙ How to contact you.
- ⊙ How to join.
- ⊙ What people can expect when they join.

It is important to give people the impression that your group is friendly, interesting, active and can make a difference. Think about your public image. The greatest control over your image lies in your own written materials. What are the impressions you want to convey to people? What language describes your group? Key words could include: lively, stimulating, inspiring, friendly, fun, and successful. Part 3 on Publicity, gives more guidance about this.

While you want to assure potential new members that your group is well-informed, avoid coming across as remote and intellectual. Your very 'ordinariness' should be one of your strongest assets.

Tip More members also means more time and effort looking after them. Focus on why you want more people to join and what your group has to offer them.

3 Making meetings work... with time for fun too

You've advertised your first public meeting and are expecting new people to turn up – so what reception are they going to get? Meetings are your public face. At a meeting you will be judged by people who are interested in your campaign. If people come to one meeting and never again, your meetings are not working for new people. And if your meetings are not working for new people, they are probably falling well short of the needs of the rest of the group too.

Group meetings should:

- ⊙ Provide an opportunity to review recent events and progress.
- ⊙ Introduce new ideas and topics.
- ⊙ Enable a discussion and exchange of views.
- ⊙ Involve people in forward planning of events/campaigns.
- ⊙ Provide a focal point for action both by experienced and newer campaigners.
- ⊙ Deal with urgent group business.
- ⊙ Allow like-minded people to socialise.
- ⊙ Be fun.

Time well spent

Regular campaign meetings should be the most effective time your group spends together. Making your meetings work effectively – for everyone – is a clear sign that your group is thinking ahead, wants to succeed in its campaigns, and is attracting new members. Developing a standard yet flexible format for meetings will allow your group to do everything it wants, and needs, to do in two hours and still have time for an after meeting social/drink. A sample meeting format is outlined in Useful tips on page 95.

Good meetings are vital. They can make all the difference between a group feeling motivated and dynamic or a group getting stuck in a rut. The success of your group meetings is in your control.

From the frontline

"One woman told me that she had been put off our meetings because they seemed so dull and lacking in purpose. She had all but given up on Ealing Friends of the Earth, but after reading in the local paper about one of our "Don't Choke Ealing" events had decided to come just one more time. This time she found the new meeting format so good that she wanted to take part in our campaign." **Christine Eborall, Ealing Friends of the Earth**

⊙⊙⊙ Top Tips ⊙⊙⊙

Good habits in meetings

- ⊙ Allow people to introduce themselves, not just give their names.
- ⊙ Make sure there is a clear agenda for all to see.
- ⊙ Recap on recent events/last meeting.
- ⊙ Keep it interesting and relevant.
- ⊙ Keep a balance of fun mixed with work.
- ⊙ Maintain variety.
- ⊙ Encourage participation at all times so that everyone can get involved and contribute to the meeting.
- ⊙ Make sure people know how the meeting works.
- ⊙ Try to keep your discussions positive.
- ⊙ Ensure the meeting (and sessions within meeting) finishes on time.
- ⊙ Make clear decisions with action points for a variety of people.
- ⊙ People should go away feeling empowered and knowing where to get more advice.
- ⊙ Make sure the venue for your meeting is accessible and there are clear directions.
- ⊙ Make sure your meeting is well planned and publicised.
- ⊙ Keep the atmosphere welcoming and friendly.

4 Getting organised: the basics of setting up a group

Now that people are interested and working together, the next step is to establish a campaign group. Getting your organisation right will make your campaigning more effective — it will help your group achieve objectives, save time, win campaigns and thrive in the longer term. Time spent now on getting the best structure for your group will pay off many times in the future. There is no 'right way' to run a group, but there will be a good way to run your group. There are legal and constitutional issues to consider when setting up a group and these are explained in Useful tips on page 96.

Campaigning requires team work

Being part of a campaign group can be hard work. You do not always see success as quickly as you might like to as most people are fitting in their campaigning around other demands such as work and family life. To keep a group running it is important that you work as a team.

Have realistic expectations Know what people can do and what they might expect. Wanting to involve more people can be code for, "This campaign needs more people like me." Successful campaigns require many different skills and tasks and the sooner this is recognised, the sooner your group will have a campaign team.

A good campaign team is a diverse campaign team

Have a common sense of purpose Set clear goals, be focussed in your campaigning work and do a few things well, rather than a lot of things in a rush.

Have a common sense of identity Ensure all group members understand how the group is set up and works, and who they need to contact about what.

Encourage involvement Encourage people to be active and voice their opinion; allow people to make mistakes; welcome new members and introduce them to other members of the group and most important of all, listen.

Value everyone's contributions Not everyone wants to be on TV or confront their local official. Offering to run a stall or shake a collecting can are equally vital to the well-being of a group. Don't forget to thank people – however small the contribution.

Recognise limitations Some people may struggle to find a spare half hour to spend on a campaign, while others may have several free days. Recognise and acknowledge that everyone has occasions when the rest of their life has to take precedence.

Make time for fun Social events should not be under-estimated. Apart from building team trust and raising funds, socials can help attract new members and allow for more informal recruitment.

Who is in charge here?

Groups can fail if one job involves far too much work – which tends to be either the chair or co-ordinator. Avoid depending on one person. It is unfair to the individual concerned, may lead to them doing a bad job or burning out, and can disempower other members of the group. An active campaign group could divide the co-ordinator role between two people. Useful appointments include:

A campaigns co-ordinator who co-ordinates the work of small task-groups (if they exist) or individual campaigners; represents the group externally (eg, on council forums or in the media); monitors media coverage; oversees the group's strategy and steers new members towards appropriate campaigns.

A group organiser who receives information on behalf of the group and distributes it promptly; is the first point of contact with the public; maintains group resources; ensures that meetings are recorded and action points followed up and steers new members towards appropriate organisational jobs.

Other potential roles include a **press officer, membership secretary** and a **treasurer** – the role of a treasurer is outlined in part 2, page 39. Another way to organise your group is to split roles into individual tasks – which means more than one person can do what would otherwise be one person's job.

(☉ Tip) Structure your group to meet your campaign needs.

What are the rules?

The formal rules about how a group is run are known as a constitution. As well as rules for running the group, a constitution should include details of the aims and objectives, membership arrangements, standing orders and the Annual General Meeting (AGM). Having a constitution ensures that there is accountability within your group. For groups starting up, a simple statement of aims should be enough to begin with. Once the group is up and running your group should agree a constitution – see Useful tips, page 97 for a model constitution.

What do we want to do?

At the first few meetings it is important to focus on being active. Activity and early successes build a sense of purpose within your campaign group, can attract more people to your cause, and show your mettle as a campaigning group. So initially don't be over-concerned with getting posts filled with the ideal candidate; instead, focus on doing things. Group work involves dozens of different jobs which are best filled by people who are both able and willing to fill them. In order to manage your group effectively find out as much as possible about your membership. This need not be a major exercise. Honest answers from group members to the following questions will give you all the management information you need:

How would you describe your skills and experience? This question pinpoints the specific tasks that people can do and how much experience they have got doing them. Do not limit this to current group activities. Ask people to list everything they can think of – you will be surprised at what you discover.

What do you want to do / feel comfortable doing? People often end up doing jobs that they do not like or feel uncomfortable with. Matching people's wishes with their role in the group means that they are more likely to do a good job and stick around.

How much time can you commit to the group? There is nothing worse than asking people to do too much. It can make individuals feel resentful, in turn demotivating other members of the group, and running the risk of driving people away.

What needs to be done?

The next step is to define the actual jobs to be done by having an open discussion with the group. Start with a long list of what jobs could be done and then prioritise this with what jobs must be done.

Write up the list of priority jobs on a large sheet of paper. When your group meeting comes to discuss how it should organise and structure itself, ask people to look at the sheet and put their names down for any roles and tasks. If this is done during a short break, people will not feel pressurised to volunteer. Several people may be willing to help with the same area of work, making sharing out tasks much easier.

Do this and your group will benefit. Giving members a stake in the organisation of your group ensures they take responsibility for the jobs that they sign up to do. The group itself gets a tailor-made structure geared towards achieving its objectives. New members will be able to see where they can fit in and can get involved more easily. Having room for those who are not 'instant' volunteers and campaigners is a good way of building a broad-based team with people to 'understudy' and step in if and when others fall away.

O Tip A well-structured group makes for a happier set of members who should be able to achieve results for years to come.

5 Staying organised: managing group dynamics

A well-structured group which holds regular well-run meetings is vital for successful campaigning. Over time, as the group works together, there will be highs and lows: highs as your campaign gets in the local press, your elected representative backs your campaign and more and more new faces turn up at weekly meetings. And there will be lows where it feels like the campaign is going nowhere and group members start to drift away. While you cannot anticipate every situation, you can manage them by preparing for busy and quiet periods of activity. Ideally:

Plan ahead The dynamics of a group constantly change. You never know when someone is going to decide to take on more work, or when a long-standing campaigner may leave. By planning ahead and giving all levels of membership something to do you will give everyone the opportunity to be involved and stay active.

Review progress when you are stuck in a rut If your campaign seems to be getting stuck, involve people in a review process. What is good about the campaign? What is not so good? What is within your group's control to change and what is not? What could be done differently?

Review progress annually As well as on-going progress reviews, hold an Annual General Meeting (AGM). This is a good opportunity to reflect on successes and look to the year ahead.

Recognise success Value achievements and successes. If the campaign gets press coverage or if there has been a successful fundraising event – share it within the group. If someone has written a good leaflet or balanced the books – tell them so!

Managing your membership

Members come and go so always be on the lookout for new blood. Public meetings and events are good places to recruit members. Build on your group's successes and keep your messages locally relevant in order to attract members.

Public meetings When you are holding or attending public meetings to rally support and publicise your campaign, build in time to call for more active and general support. Advertising tasks for specific roles on large sheets of paper — such as "Wanted" posters — is one way of allowing people to approach you, as well as allowing you to target specific skills.

Events Early on, you may want to set up an event with the aim of getting media coverage for your campaign. Build in a call for new members and if you know the event is definitely being covered by the local paper/radio/TV, follow it up with letters to local papers about your campaign, ending by asking for help and funds. Part 4 page 63 explains how to go about organising an event.

Build on success People are attracted to groups that are seen to be successful. When dealing with members of the public — whether in face-to-face discussions or through written materials — be positive and sell your successes. As the saying goes, nothing succeeds like success.

Always be on the lookout for new members

Be relevant If you are trying to attract people to a campaign on climate change, when the biggest local campaign issue is an incineration plant, then this will limit your local appeal. Know your local issues and take account of them in group decisions about what sort of campaign to run.

Managing people

Groups are made up of individuals and there are practical ways to manage and support individuals to get the best out of your group.

Work together Even if your group is working well in small groups, identify one job that everyone can do together. Whether it's stuffing envelopes, painting banners or a group outing, it can be motivating – and fun – to plan an activity involving everyone.

Be realistic Everyone has to start somewhere. The more realistic and specific you are about what tasks involve, the less daunting they are to people.

Develop skills Improve group/individual's skills through, for example, creating opportunities for constructive feedback within your group. What about using outsiders' skills? Would campaigners or experts be willing to visit your group for an evening and talk about how they succeeded?

Develop confidence Confident campaigners are not necessarily born, but made through experience. Encourage more experienced people to work with newer people and show them the ropes, or get more experienced campaigners to explain issues to the group.

Managing difficult times

During its lifetime your group may experience some sort of internal friction, and if it is not resolved it can become a distraction from campaigning or even a negative force within the group. Dealing with internal differences is not pleasant and unfortunately there is no magic wand to spirit them away. Basic suggestions to help include:

Bring the issue into the open Ignoring it will only make it worse, as will moaning about it in smaller groups. Avoid making any assumptions on behalf of anyone else – state what you see as the issue and say how this affects you. An issue with the group is best addressed to the group, while an issue with an individual is best addressed to the person concerned initially.

Propose a mechanism for discussing and resolving the issue This should be an open and non-confrontational way of discussing the matter, taking into account all relevant information and involving everyone with an interest. It should reach a clear outcome that people agree to, even if this is a process for resolving the issue at a later stage.

Do not be afraid to make hard decisions

You cannot please everyone all of the time. If your group has genuinely taken everyone's view into account, and reaches a decision that it believes to be fair and that best enables the group to achieve its objectives, then you must carry through that decision no matter how unattractive it may seem at the time – you will not regret it.

From the frontline

Sometimes things don't always go smoothly for local campaigning groups. Problems can arise when people who were originally very active in a group decide it is time for them to move on to other things. In Brighton and Hove Friends of the Earth's case when the key campaigner needed to reduce his activities it became clear that the group needed to take ownership of the situation and decide what to do next.

"The first step was to recognise that there was a problem!" said Paul Mason, one of the group members. "To work out exactly what this problem was, we got an impartial facilitator to attend the next monthly meeting. Having an impartial view allowed us to identify the key problems and come up with ideas about how to move the group forward. Luckily, there was sufficient enthusiasm and experience to realise that by changing a few simple things (such as the way meetings are run) the group could start to revitalise itself. While solutions may not be instant, we are now beginning to develop new campaigns and strategies for the future."

Building your campaign Part 2
How to find focus, friends and funds

1 Drawing up a campaign plan

A campaign plan should help increase your group's chances of success and identify the most effective course of action to take. In real life nothing is straightforward. Situations change rapidly, and campaign plans need to be redesigned as necessary. Useful tips, page 99 gives an example of a campaign plan based on the following basic steps:

Decide on your campaign aim and objectives Your aim spells out what the campaign wants to achieve overall. You should be able to sum this aim up in one clear sentence, eg, "Stop the road". An aim should be realistic and achievable.

Always make sure your aims are realistic and achievable

The objectives are the building blocks by which your campaign aim is achieved. Objectives are most useful when they are SMART — that is, they are:

SMART Campaign objectives

Specific	Measurable	Achievable	Realistic	Time-specific
Stop Toxico local factory fouling our air.	See a 10 per cent reduction in Toxico's emissions.	This has been successful before.	I know we can do this.	We can do this in one year.
Not Stop local pollution.	Not Mmm...less pollution?	Not Hard to say without being specific.	Not I think we could do this.	Not This will takes ages.

25

Identify your targets All campaign objectives will have targets: the people or institutions which can bring about the changes you are campaigning for. Examples of targets include industry; manufacturers; producers; companies; retailers; the general public (perhaps as consumers, or voters) and political decision makers (local, regional, national, European or international). A strong campaign needs strong demands so you need to be clear about what you want your targets to do.

Develop your key messages Once you have identified your targets, develop key campaign messages. Always check that your messages are based directly on your aims and objectives, and that they sum up your demands clearly. Work out which slogans you recall from adverts – why do they stick in your memory? A successful campaign message is one people remember. See Part 3 for more information on basic publicity.

There are lots of ways to communicate key messages including badges, stickers, posters, fliers, newsletters, interviews, press releases, information packs, fact sheets, e-mail and websites. Make sure your communications contain solutions, and not just complaints or criticisms about the problems. Where you can, try and offer acceptable, alternative proposals as ways out for your targets.

Know your facts Make sure you're familiar with the issues and know your facts – see page 77 for details.

Choose your tactics Your choice of tactics depends not only on who your target is, but on the issue, the timing, what stage the campaign is at, opportunities for influence and how much pressure you want to apply. For example you can use consumer pressure, stunts, demonstrations, street theatre, public meetings and debates, consultations, public inquiries, lobbying your elected representative, street stalls, petitions, letter writing, using famous people/local celebrities for your media work, exhibitions, surveys, environmental monitoring, launching a report and peaceful protest.

Mobilise the public The majority of campaigns are won because of public pressure. Look for easy, straightforward ways the public can get involved in your campaign, and include them as points about "How you can take action" on every leaflet/briefing. You can also use campaign postcards and petitions to engage the public, and give them a chance to take part in creating change.

Develop a media strategy The media is an essential channel for reaching your targets. When planning campaigns, consider how to use the media to get your messages across, and gain maximum exposure at prime opportunities. See Part 4 page 57 on how to get to know the media and use it to your group's advantage.

Draw up schedules for main activities/events Draw up rough timings on what needs to be done in the next year and identify when your major events should be. Working backwards from these key dates, you should be able to put together a work plan. For example a public meeting in three months time requires forward planning:

- ⊙ Month 1: Plan the venue and book the speakers.
- ⊙ Month 2: Promote it through posters and leaflets.
- ⊙ Month 3: Do media work.

Draw up a summary of what needs to happen by when – with clear priorities. Estimate the length of time it will take to achieve each action step, and add 10 to 20 per cent extra for the unexpected. You will almost always need it. See Part 4, page 63 about how to run a great event.

Know who your allies are, and work with them Who else is doing something similar to you? Can you link up with other community groups which are already doing similar activities? Working with allies can be invaluable when there are lots of good ideas and not enough people to make them happen. The next section, on page 28, tells you how to go about networking with other groups.

Identify fundraising opportunities Every campaign opportunity is a possible fundraising opportunity. Make sure you use public meetings and talks to collect money, have collecting tins on street stalls, and add requests for donations in your leaflets and publications. Consider what resources are needed for each stage of the campaign, and plan how to get hold of them as easily and cheaply as possible. Fundraising tips are outlined on page 34.

Review, evaluate and monitor your campaign When and how will you judge whether the campaign has been successful? Are you on the right path for success? Periodic monitoring and evaluation will help you decide whether to change tack, or keep going in the same direction. For example if your local authority has taken some of your concerns on board but instead of scrapping the road scheme, is just changing the route, reassess your campaign plan.

Draw out the strengths in your successes, and be honest about weak links in your campaign. Use this information to change direction if necessary. Set aside times when you will review, evaluate and monitor your campaign plan – do not leave it until the campaign is over. See Useful tips, page 99.

"We won!"

When you do have a campaign victory, take time to celebrate your success. Victories are significant milestones, and marking them can re-energise your campaign. Always be prepared to win, even when you think it is very unlikely – you can do this by being ready with the victory press release should a decision go your way. Winning campaigns can become infectious, and it has got to be one of the best ways of attracting new members to your group.

⊘ Tip A successful campaign is one that is strategically focussed and planned.

2 Networking in the real world

The more a campaign becomes representative of a significant volume of people and interests, the greater it is likely to succeed. Building links and associations with people and organisations in the community adds to your local relevance, as well as increasing the support base for your campaign.

Networking involves getting the message out about your group – its aims, objectives and current campaigns – to like-minded groups. For example, a campaign on local air pollution might be able to tap into local residents' groups, mother and toddler groups, a local cycling campaign and so on. Networking should be an on-going activity which can spread your message and build support within local organisations in your community.

Alliances are more formal and focussed, where you may ask organisations to work alongside you for a specific campaign with a defined time scale. For example, community groups across the Midlands joined forces to try and stop the Birmingham Northern Relief Road. In the campaign to stop the East London River Crossing (and Save Oxleas Wood) a number of organisations joined forces to add clout and legitimacy to the campaign. Overall the decision to join or form an alliance will be determined by your campaign strategy.

Networking

Where to start The first step is to investigate local campaigning and community organisations. Your local library or voluntary resources centre will have a directory of community groups – think laterally and do not just go for the usual suspects. Discuss networking opportunities at a group meeting so that you can identify which organisations to focus on and contact. Networking can help you to fill specific skills gaps, such as legal, planning and IT skills by bringing these in from other organisations. You may also be able to target and fill specific resource needs, such as computers, printing facilities and local materials.

Making that initial contact Once you have identified groups which might be interested in your campaign, make contact, first in writing, enclosing copies of campaign materials such as leaflets and briefings. Then follow this up with a telephone call asking them whether they want to support your campaign and if so how. For example:

- ⊙ Would they like someone to talk to their group about the campaign?
- ⊙ Would they be willing to distribute information to their membership?
- ⊙ Would they like to go on your campaign mailing list?
- ⊙ Would they like to support your campaign by signing a petition?

Tapping into existing networks As well as looking at organisations, look out for networks that are up and running. Such networks often charge a membership fee, but in return you may get a newsletter, access to advice and training. You will be tapping into an existing pool of skills and expertise and can ask – as a member – to contribute articles for network newsletters, an efficient and fast way to get your message out to many more people. For example the West Midlands Environment Network acts as a networking forum for information exchange, the sharing of resources, and the provision of support to enable groups, organisations and individuals across the West Midlands region to communicate more effectively. It works to strengthen the links between organisations and help people to make new contacts, set up new projects and gives advice on working in partnership with others. It is particularly involved in supporting the Local Agenda 21 process in the region. As a member you get a monthly newsletter and, access to information, resources and training.

Alliances

Alliances often form around single-issue campaigns such as a school closure, new incinerator, road proposal or landfill site. The actual aims of some groups may be different but on this particular issue there may be common ground. Forming an alliance can further your campaign by allowing you to:

⊙ Cover campaign targets more effectively.

⊙ Campaign effectively – involving other groups can increase your choice of campaign tactics and bring diverse voices to the campaign.

⊙ Delegate to a bigger pool of differing experience and interests.

⊙ Develop a wide skills and knowledge base, as well as sharing your resources, eg, reports and exhibitions.

⊙ Be seen to be co-operating, not going it alone.

⊙ Develop credibility in your community.

But there are also potential drawbacks to working in alliances:

⊙ Your group can become invisible by getting swallowed up by the alliance and lose sight of its own group identity or campaign objectives.

⊙ A lot of time can be wasted on trying to achieve consensus between groups with different agendas.

⊙ Groups may find themselves with strange bedfellows, such as a local politician trying to gain popularity through association with the alliance.

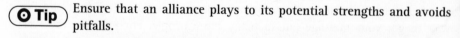 Ensure that an alliance plays to its potential strengths and avoids pitfalls.

Have one very specific aim The simple single rule of an alliance is to have one specific aim, such as "No School Closure" or "Yes to Mytown Wind Farm". This makes it easy for groups and individuals to join the campaign and will stop internal debates about alternatives that may be on offer.

Agree an identity Some alliances opt for a common identity, such as an alliance logo, with all materials accordingly branded – leaflets, newsletters, reports, banners. Internally, groups represent their own organisations and agree actions. Externally, the campaign – public meetings, media work, etc, – is done in the name of the alliance. Another option is for groups to keep their separate identities and co-ordinate their work through the alliance. Whichever option your group chooses, alliance members need to discuss it, agree it and stick to it.

Set ground rules Are you going to work on everything together or only on specific parts of the campaign? At times it makes sense to work together; at times you may have a stronger impact by working individually. How are you going to handle press enquiries – is anyone going to do it or do you need to agree two or three people who will lead on press work? How are you going to handle the finances? Setting ground rules from the outset will head off many of the potential problems of working in alliances.

Agree an end point Your campaign may be won or lost. Either way the time will come when it makes sense to disband. Be prepared to recognise when the role of the alliance has come to an end.

From the frontline

The Birmingham Northern Relief Road (BNRR), if built, will be Britain's first toll motorway, running from Junction 4 of the M6 near Coleshill, Warwickshire to north of Junction 11 near Cannock in Staffordshire. People in the area have been fighting against a road for more than 17 years. Hazel Barnes and her husband John moved to the area and immediately took action to stop the road being built. *"Everyone in the village was concerned but nobody seemed to be doing anything about it. So John and I started a local petition,"* she says. Initially the campaign was being fought by many residential and community groups in different villages. *"It wasn't until the first Public Inquiry in 1988 that we realised that there were so many groups fighting the same campaign. We had lots of common ground and realised that we could do far more if we worked together,"* adds Hazel.

After the second inquiry (1994-1995) The Alliance Against the BNRR was born, with one simple aim: to stop the road. Hazel Barnes, now a spokesperson for the Alliance, summed up why the partnership is crucial to the success of the campaign. *"The Alliance has meant that our campaigning is more focussed and has brought together people with lots of different skills. This campaign is so important. It is showing the Government and the business world that people will not accept road schemes which will bring nothing but misery to the area."*

3 Networking in the virtual world

Networking is not just about face-to-face contact and spreading paper information. More and more people are using electronic communications as a way to get and share information fast. Electronic communication is becoming an increasingly important campaign tool, enabling groups to put their campaigning on a stronger footing and save time.

At the touch of a button

Would you like to be in regular contact with people across the country who are campaigning on your issue? E-mail offers this opportunity – it is fast, easy to use and inexpensive. Campaigners who use e-mail are sharing up-to-date information, generating ideas and campaign tactics, swapping their experiences of previous campaigns and benefiting from mutual support.

A further benefit is the wide range of e-mail networks (known as lists or discussion groups) that are set up to share information on specific campaign issues. By subscribing to an e-mail network – at no cost – you will receive mailings from other people who share your campaign interests, and you will be able to contact all of them with just one touch of a button.

E-mail is now a campaign tactic in its own right. You can send a message to almost any campaign target, from the US White House or multinational companies down to your local authority or developer. What is more, it can be easier to co-ordinate an e-mail campaign than a letter writing or faxing campaign. To get hold of someone's e-mail address – ask them directly or do a "search" on the internet.

The mother of all libraries

The world wide web is potentially the largest source of information in the world. Almost everyone now publishes information there: governments, companies and academic institutions as well as campaign groups and individuals. Whatever you want to know, no matter how specialist, there is a good chance that you will find it on the web. Through "search engines" on the web you can type in a name or description and are instantly given matches. It is like having the mother of all libraries in your front room. The web is a place where you can publish your own information as well (see Part 4 page 72).

It won't break the bank

Electronic communication is relatively cheap, and access is getting cheaper as the real cost of hardware comes down and more internet service providers offer free services. Using e-mail (without web access) does not require much computer memory and is practical on a bottom-of the-range or second-hand machine. The cost of an e-mail account is roughly half that of full access to the web (if you pay at all) and as most e-mails are sent or received in a few seconds, via a local number, it will not make a huge difference to your telephone bill.

Using the web can be more costly. You will need a more powerful machine to do this efficiently, and despite calls being charged at the local rate, hours of "surfing" will make a difference to your phone bill. But free or low-cost access to electronic communication is becoming more widely available. Libraries, community centres, colleges and cyber cafes are among the venues, and there are also companies that will give you a free e-mail account.

Go on, give it a go

If you are tempted by what electronic communication can offer, why not at least give it a try? There is bound to be somewhere locally to do this, or a friend or family member might show you how. Better still, sign up for one of the many adult education classes for Information Technology (IT) novices and learn how to get the most out of a computer.

 Electronic communication is the future. As campaigners we can seize the future right now, and take advantage of the many benefits that the information age brings to our campaigning.

From the frontline

"I have found the internet incredibly useful in my campaigning against organochlorine pollution, mainly through my use of e-mail lists. I subscribe to an e-mail list which is dedicated to toxic chemicals. Through the list, I can keep up to date with the latest news and technical information, and I can pick the brains of others on the list, who include scientists, consultants and other activists.

"Recently I was looking for solutions to decontaminating a local area which was originally used as dredging lagoons but is now fields. I was trying to find out the latest, greenest technology to remedy this sort of soil contamination. By coincidence, a

33

campaigner in the US e-mailed a new report on this topic to a colleague of mine. Through e-mail, I was able to contact the author, ask for permission to quote it, and whether I could have several printed copies to give out. E-mail has enabled me to have a copy of the report on my computer and on my desk within minutes instead of days – at the cost of a local phone call. It is absolutely invaluable."

Viv Mountford, Halton Friends of the Earth Local Group

4 Getting the money

The first rule of fundraising is that, "You don't get what you don't ask for". Do not be afraid to ask for funds to run your campaigns. After all, if you are trying to do something for the good of your community then why should you feel awkward about asking for money to make it happen? There are several ways of raising money for your campaign and they are not all mutually exclusive. For example you can organise a fundraising event, hold a street collection, run a raffle or fundraise from trusts.

Organising a fundraising event

A good fundraising event can help to recruit new members, publicise an issue and raise funds. It is important to plan ahead and get as much publicity for the idea as you can. Be creative and try to put a campaign spin on your fundraising. Most importantly, make things fun so that everyone enjoys taking part.

Decide objectives before organising an fundraising event If you do this, every subsequent decision will be easier. With clear objectives in mind you can decide what sort of event you want to run, when, where and how many people need to get involved. Try and set objectives that can be measured, for example you may want to raise £500 and recruit 20 new members before the end of October. Make sure that any event idea you come up with is fun and meets the objectives you have set. If it does not seem to do this, look again at your objectives and ask yourself are they reasonable?

Consider when is the best time to hold your event Think also about what other local events might conflict with yours. Also consider the wider implications of the date you choose, eg, school holidays, bank holiday weekends and big sporting events such as the World Cup.

Event ideas

A sale These are easy to organise and can raise a lot of money. The stall could be at a fair or local fête, a car boot sale, plant sale, book sale, jumble sale or theme market. To run a successful sale:

- ⊙ Decide on the best venue to hold the sale and get permission as necessary.
- ⊙ Publicise and promote the sale as much as possible.
- ⊙ Get together with friends and relatives to collect items to sell well in advance.
- ⊙ Make the stall look as attractive and welcoming as you can.

Sponsored events These are a great way to raise money and can be a lot of fun. How about a sponsored sports event, walk, swimathon or bike ride? Or you could clean up your local environment with a sponsored litter pick. These are just a few of the more usual ideas. Think up more outlandish ones and they will attract more publicity, people and money.

Other ideas Pub quiz, medieval banquet, talent show, open garden day, painting and cookery, cabaret, cake bake, second-hand book sale, treasure hunt, bicycle tour, cricket/football match, Monopoly tournament, wine/ale/cider/whisky tasting evening, theme party, horror walk, board games night at a local pub. The list is endless but only you can come up with the one most suited to your area, contacts and members.

Street collections

Street collections are particularly valuable. Not only do they generate vital funds, but the sight of collectors on the streets can create greater awareness of your work in the best way possible – by meeting people face to face. A street collection can raise a lot of money if you plan it well and generate sufficient interest. Here's how:

- ⊙ Appoint one person to act as co-ordinator for the collection.
- ⊙ A collection is best organised well in advance. Once you have chosen a date, apply to the local licensing authority – usually the police or the County Council – for a permit. (Note: in Northern Ireland street collection permits are issued by the police – see Useful reading on page 108 for details of how to get hold of information on campaigning in Northern Ireland). They will have a standard application form – and

it is best submitted well in advance. If collecting on private property, you must have written permission from the owner.

⊙ Once a permit has been issued it is important that you read the regulations accompanying it carefully.

⊙ Collect where as many people as possible pass by. Work out all the most strategic places and how many people you will need to cover them. Popular locations include high streets and shopping centres.

⊙ The co-ordinator must ensure that all cans are accounted for and proceeds recorded in the manner instructed by your licensing authority. Detailed accounts need to be returned to the authority after the collection, and failure to do so will prevent future permits being issued.

⊙ Once proceeds have been counted, why not end the day on a high note by holding a thank you party for everyone involved?

Raffles

Raffles are fun to organise and easy to promote – not least because you can offer a tangible incentive for everyone to take part. Issues to consider when planning your raffle:

Consult the Gaming Board Raffles must comply with strict regulations from the Gaming Board of Great Britain (see Useful contacts, page 105). In Northern Ireland the district council is responsible for registering lotteries and raffles – contact the Department of Social Development on 028 905 22607 for information about regulations.

Source some prizes Prizes are important but they do not need to cost a lot. Ideally, get them donated. It should not be hard to find a friendly local business that would be happy to let you have a food hamper or two, gift tokens or free tickets to a local event.

Print and produce tickets Printing up tickets can take some time and you will need to research the most cost-effective method of production. Their style and design will depend on what you can afford. All tickets must be numbered and you must keep a record of who is selling and buying them. There must be space for a name and address or telephone number on each ticket stub.

Distribute tickets You can sell tickets at local fêtes and any of the events mentioned previously. If you have a newsletter, how about distributing them with that? Local public outlets may be prepared to sell them on their counter. Keep an accurate record of who you have got to help you.

Fundraising from trusts

Funding is available from both private and public sources. These include the National Lottery Charities Board, charitable trusts and companies. Contact details are listed on page 106. Also see Useful reading on page 108.

⊙⊙⊙ Top Tips ⊙⊙⊙

Successful fundraising events

Delegate as much as possible Set up an event committee and allocate tasks.

Advance planning If you are organising a fundraising event, set a deadline so that if you have not yet arranged everything (sold enough tickets/arranged sponsorship/got that free venue you need) you have time to cancel or postpone the event. It is important to be objective about this. Cancelling any event brings disappointment, but if things are not going to work out then being a bit ruthless will save embarrassment (and money) later on. There is nothing more demoralising than waiting for the people that never turn up.

Selling tickets If you are selling tickets, keep a record initially of ticket numbers and where books of tickets have been distributed for sale. Directly before the event collect all the unsold tickets to avoid any problems with tickets falling into the wrong hands. If the event is cancelled, depending on the scale of the event it is appropriate to reimburse ticket price, less any advance booking fee. Make clear at the time of sale the procedure by which tickets will be reimbursed if the event should be cancelled.

There are more than 20,000 grant-making trusts and foundations in the UK. These organisations distribute around £1 billion a year to good causes. Most of these funds are controlled by the top 1,000 trusts, which mainly give to national organisations, but there are a significant number of very local grant-making bodies. The Directory of Social Change produces guides about local trusts and ways to fundraise (see Useful contacts, page 105). For fundraising advice and information about trusts in Northern Ireland and Wales contact the relevant Council for Voluntary Action (see Useful contacts, page 106).

The above are a few ways in which you can raise funds and increase membership. If you set up a new fundraising initiative make sure you are aware of any relevant legislation before you start. Fundraising laws centre around not being a nuisance to the public — know the law and stay within it.

From the frontline

At low tide Morecambe Bay is a vast expanse of sand stretching from Morecambe on the south to the shores of Cumbria in the north. Before the advent of the railways crossing the bay, on foot or by horse, was a normal part of the journey from Lancaster to Grange, Cartmel or Ulverston. North Lancashire Friends of the Earth thought that a sponsored 'crossing the bay' walk, sounded like an easy and enjoyable way to raise money, and could be used to highlight some of the environmental issues associated with the bay, such as the pollution of the sands by radioactivity from Sellafield, and the potential future sea level rise caused by global warming.

Anne Chapman, co-ordinator of the group, explains how they went about raising the money. *"We had to do some organisation beforehand. The most important thing was widespread publicity. We printed lots of posters and distributed them about the town; made sure we were in local events guides, and the newspapers. We decided to make a charge of £5 for those who did not want to collect sponsorship. On the day more than 100 people turned out and we all had a great time. After paying the guide £50 we made a handsome profit of more than £400. This money is vital for the day-to-day running of our group and we will be able to use it to support our local campaigning work on food issues."*

5 Managing the money

Once the money starts to roll in, you'll need to think about how to manage it. There are financial and legal issues to consider. For example, there is a legal obligation to record all monies received and notes must be kept of who has given personal donations. Also, if you are on the street asking for funds, you must carry some form of ID, such as a letter from your group saying that you are fundraising for them. To help manage the finances of your group you need to make some formal decisions.

Appoint a treasurer

Many groups have a constitution which requires a treasurer to be appointed as a minimum for the group to be considered functional (see Useful tips, page 96). It is wise to draw up a job description, stating what the minimum requirements of the post are. When appointing a treasurer ask for a reference from someone who can vouch for their honesty. It is also useful to give clear guidelines about what information about the group's finances will be required, for example at group meetings.

Appoint a treasurer

The treasurer does not have to be a professional accountant but will have to keep a record of the money going in and out. This is needed so that the finances of the group are kept in order and so that there is proof that the funds are being spent properly.

Money is a temptation and this can lead to theft. Issuing minimum requirements through a job description or written code of conduct enables a group to legitimately ask a treasurer to leave if it is necessary.

Banking basics

Get a bank account Groups need to open a bank account to receive funds – this avoids the potential problem of money going missing from a personal bank account. Two people will be needed as signatories. You may want to choose a bank with a more ethical stance. Banks have varying criteria for business accounts: some require a minimum balance, others restrict access so it's worth shopping around and presenting findings to the group for them to decide. The bank will issue a cheque book and a paying-in book – make sure you ask for regular monthly statements. Remember that the officers (ie, treasurer, group organiser) of your campaign group may be held responsible for actions of the group if the group goes into debt. So avoid this situation.

Get two account books It helps to track cash flows by having one for bank transactions – your campaign account – and one for cash transactions – your petty cash. Cash books can be bought from stationers.

Get a receipt book All payments should be accompanied by a receipt. This helps to make sure money is not stolen.

High tech There are a number of useful word processing packages which can be used to keep a record of your group's accounts.

Recording your finances

When you start your campaign account book or your petty cash account book decide on a recording system which works. A simple method is to write on the top of the left hand page "Incoming Money" and on the top of the right "Outgoing Money". Then on the left hand page record (date, details and amount) incoming money, eg, donations, in date order. On the right hand page record the date you paid out any money, what the payment was for and how much.

When you receive or pay out money Record it at once and write out a receipt.

File receipts Keep all receipts in an envelope, filed or clipped together.

Petty cash

When you need money in your hand, for example to deal with small expenses such as stamps, withdraw money from your campaign account and mark it as a petty cash withdrawal under "Outgoing Money". In your petty cash book this

Good financial housekeepng

- Pay all money received into the bank. Confusion arises when cash is received and then paid out without ever being recorded.
- Keep all receipts and invoices. Make sure you keep and file all invoices and receipts.
- Record cheques; make sure the cheque counterfoil gives details of the payee, amount and type of expense (travel, printing etc).
- Get someone else to double check. If the books are not balanced, a different pair of eyes may spot something in five minutes that you have been looking at for hours.

would be recorded as "Incoming Money". Then any cash you spend is recorded under "Outgoing Money" in the petty cash book. Receipts should be kept in the same way as for your campaign account.

Balancing the books
At the end of the month or quarter, balance the books. Add up the receipts and payments. The balance is the total receipts, less the total payments.

Annual accounts
The point of balancing the books is to make sure that at the end of the financial year the group's account books and bank account tally. For small groups it may be enough for a treasurer to produce an end of year accounts statement, together with the account books and the bank's statements for inspection at your Annual General Meeting. If you are receiving funding from an outside source then you will probably be asked to have audited accounts. This involves an accountant officially checking your banks details and books and writing a certificate confirming that they are correct. Consider asking a friend, or looking for someone who is a practicing or retired accountant to do this for you.

Managing money from events

Money, especially cash should be banked as soon as possible. Make sure basic checks are made at the time to ensure larger currency is genuine (eg, £20 and £50 notes), and check the following on personal cheques:

⊙ Is the guarantee card valid? Check the expiry date.

⊙ Signature; does it match signature on banker's card?

⊙ Is the date correct? Beware of backdated cheques, which can be cancelled, and post-dated cheques, which cannot be banked immediately.

⊙ Make sure you tell people who to make any cheques payable to.

⊙ Does the amount exceed the limit specified on a banker's card?

⊙ Ask the purchaser to write their address on the back of a cheque. This could avoid problems later, and most people are happy to do so.

Legal issues

Your tax status Most voluntary groups will be characterised under the heading of "Clubs, societies and associations". Some may be registered as separate legal entities. Unfortunately there is no automatic exemption from tax. The Inland Revenue Guidance leaflet IR46 sets out the position with regard to Income and Corporation tax and can be obtained from your local tax office.

Trading Any group which regularly trades will be liable to pay tax on the profits generated through trading, irrespective of the purpose for which these profits are used. Note: trading includes the sale of publications.

Events Make sure you have sorted out all permissions and other legal requirements well in advance of the event (see pages 65 for further details). One specific responsibility is recording proceeds of a street collection with your local authority. If you are organising a street collection, ask your bank for bank bags in advance and bag up loose change in multiples of a pound, clearly marked with amounts contained (no bank appreciates customers emptying pockets of change on to the counter).

Registering raffles or lotteries You will need to register any raffles or lotteries, naming an individual in the group as the promoter. You'll also need to prepare a financial report on the outcome of your raffle or lottery. For a complete guide on raffle requirements, and for specific questions, contact your local district council's licensing officer. In Northern Ireland contact the Department of Social Development for a leaflet about the law on lotteries, on 028 905 22607.

Publicity

Part 3

Your basic tool kit

1 What's the message?

As campaigners we are competing for people's attention in a noisy, busy world and against people who have large media and advertising budgets. As campaigners we are also prone to getting so immersed in the merits of our issue that we can forget that last crucial step before we launch ourselves on to an unsuspecting public – trying to put ourselves in their shoes. You do not need a big budget to get people's attention – though it can clearly help. What you do need to do is pay attention to planning and preparation.

What do you want to say?

Before you set up a street stall or print a leaflet, ask yourself some basic questions about your communication with the public. Try to write down the basics of your message in one or two short sentences. It will help strip away all the secondary details about the issue you are working on and arrive at something snappy that will grab attention in the shortest possible time.

Imagine your audience asking: "Why are you telling me this? Why is it important?" It may seem obvious to you, but unless you explain it to someone who knows nothing about the issue, your campaign will seem small, complicated and irrelevant. And remember, you are not trying to give a technical explanation of why your issue is important. You are talking to ordinary people, not specialists. Try to remember what first grabbed you about the campaign. What made you so concerned in the first place?

Why are you telling people?

What exactly do you want people to do when they have seen your poster, read your leaflet or have visited your street stall? Whenever possible, your communications should contain a clear call to action. This could be joining your group, sending a letter, boycotting a product, donating money or attending a public event.

Who are you telling?

"The public" is a fuzzy term. People adopt many different roles and swap roles in the same week, be it as a shopper, a parent, a motorist, a bus passenger and a walker. At different times they will be receptive to different messages so your communications will be much more effective if you target specific people.

People will be receptive to different messages at different times

For example, if your message contains a health aspect, why not display leaflets at the local gym or swimming pool? If you are talking about food, the obvious place is outside a supermarket. A word of warning, though: people are bombarded by different messages every day. Do not automatically assume that people will listen to your message – or indeed care. Tell your audience quickly and clearly what they can do to help.

How are you going to tell them?

Once you have worked out who your audience is, and your basic message, decide on the best way to get your message over.

A publicity stall

A stall gives your group a visible presence and enables you to recruit members, fundraise and enlist support for your campaign. The best day for a stall is Saturday. Ensure that one person has overall responsibility and draws up a timetable for staffing the stall.

Pick a busy public spot where people have space to hang around and chat. Good places are your local high street or outside your Town Hall. If you are on a public pavement, it is a good idea to seek permission from your local council, or the Department of Regional Development Roads Service in Northern Ireland, first. They will want to check out what you are doing (note, if you are planning to shake collecting cans you need permission – see page 35) and will also want an assurance that you will not leave the high street, or wherever the stall is pitched, littered with leaflets. If you are planning your stall in a shopping centre you will need to ask permission from the shopping centre management.

- Move on if you are asked to by the police. However unless you are obstructing a public highway (see page 65), you are unlikely to encounter this problem.
- Make your stall eye-catching by using a banner as a backdrop, and a neat tablecloth.
- Make sure everything on your stall reinforces your group's core campaigning message.

Leaflets

A leaflet should grab the reader's attention and spur them into action. Leaflets are ideal for publicising specific events, or gathering support for a particular campaign action. They can also be used to encourage people to join your campaign.

Getting your message across To get your message across, you need to make your leaflet eye-catching. Write a simple but hard-hitting statement or slogan for the front page to catch people's interest, and then add an eye-catching, relevant graphic. The rest of the leaflet should back up your core message and guide the reader to a call to action.

Don't try to explain all the technical details of your campaign in the leaflet. If people want to know detailed policy, provide a briefing-sheet or report instead. It's also important to avoid jargon, acronyms like "LA21" and formula like "CO_2". Also avoid using complicated terms such as "waste hierarchy" and "eutrophication". They mean nothing to most people.

Finally, use the leaflet to advertise your group – make sure your group's logo is placed in a prominent position on the leaflet.

Posters

A poster must be able to grab a reader's attention from afar and communicate your main message instantly to convince someone to take action. Think about the most likely locations for your poster and the average distance it will be from the reader. Don't crowd the poster with copy; it is unlikely anyone will read it and your message will get lost. If you are planning for the poster to be used with other materials, eg, a leaflet, then you can keep it very simple by using just a slogan and image.

One-to-one contact

Whether running a stall, or handing out leaflets, you are in direct contact with the public — so it is a good idea to prepare what to say in advance.

Your opening line is crucial Encourage people to respond by using an open question like: "What do you think about the planned road?"

Read all your own materials If you are pushing a particular campaign, make sure your group is fully up to speed with the latest developments and background information.

Body language You should be relaxed, friendly and approachable (but try to avoid a fixed grin).

Preparation It's important that you are prepared so that you are able to answer any sticky questions you might be asked. But remember, you are trying to interest people in your campaign – not win arguments. If you cannot answer a question – take their name and contact details and promise to get back to them with an answer.

Overall

Stalls, posters and leaflets are just a few ways of communicating to the public. There are many other techniques, such as using stickers or postcards. The main thing to remember is that everything should back up your core message, be attractive, be succinct and grab attention.

 Remember, what you have to say is important, so it makes sense to spend time getting your public message exactly right.

⊙ ⊙ ⊙ Top Tips ⊙ ⊙ ⊙

Good communication

Use direct language Use specific, active words instead of generalised or vague expressions.

Keep your language active Use active language to get people's attention. One trick that keeps your language active is to use the shortest possible verb in a sentence.

Keep it short and simple Keep your sentences short. The golden rule is, if you can cut text, do it!

Be positive when you communicate Turns things around to give a positive outlook. To be positive, use the active voice, be precise, stand up and be counted.

Avoid jargon Don't assume your audience knows everything you do. If you avoid jargon, you'll keep more people with you.

Be imaginative You can get your message across through clever puns, adapted 'common sense' sayings, metaphors and rhetorical questions, eg, 'We're not choking' for a traffic campaign. But avoid clichés.

2 Designing effectively

To communicate a campaign message you need to think about how design can help you. For example, if you want to produce a leaflet, newsletter or poster your job will be to make your product so attractive that it stands out or entices someone to pick it up. You will need to make it easy to use by arranging the text and pictures so that people are guided through the publication without confusion about which section they should read, or look at, next.

Establish the brief

Whether you are designing your own materials or commissioning a designer it is important to establish what the aims of the publication are supposed to be. This is known as a brief. To do this for a poster, work out:

- ⊙ **The purpose of the poster** Is it promotional or is it going to communicate a hard-hitting message? Does it have to provoke an action?
- ⊙ **Who the poster is aimed at** You need to know whether it is being designed for a particular group or age range.
- ⊙ **Where the poster will be displayed** You may need to produce a more striking design for a poster which will be displayed in a window than one which people read on a community notice board.
- ⊙ **How the poster will be reproduced (eg, photocopying/printing?)** How many colours can you use? Are there any photographs/images that must be included? Are there any logos to be included?
- ⊙ **How people will know who is talking to them** What details, phone numbers and web addresses will be included?

Ways to tempt people to read text

Below are a few ways to encourage people to read your campaign messages.

- ⊙ **Main headline/title** This will be the largest piece of text and the first to be read. Keep it short and to the point. You should be able to do this in less than seven words.
- ⊙ **Standfirst** This is the second piece of information people will read and is used to explain the main headline. It can be longer and used to introduce the reader to the subject. Make this a smaller size than main headlines, but bigger than subheadings.
- ⊙ **Subheadings/crossheads** These are useful to break up blocks of text by introducing new sections.

- ⊙ **Body copy** This is the text containing the main bulk of information.

Other details to consider

- ⊙ **Logos** You need to decide how you want to use your logo. Do you want it to stand out or do you want to use it as a stamp to remind people who has created the poster, placard or publication?

- ⊙ **Images** From your selection of images decide whether you have one that will work well on the leaflet's cover or poster by grabbing the reader's or passer-by's attention.

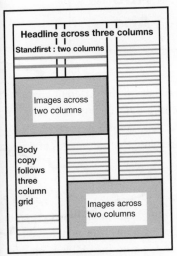

Keep the information tidy

Using a basic grid is a very helpful way of organising your information. It helps you place text and images along baselines, margins and columns. Grids are especially useful in keeping the layout consistent on publications of more then one page or on publications which are produced on a regular basis. Many desktop publishing packages have model grids which can be used or adapted.

The grid on the left shows a basic three column format. The headline spans all three columns the standfirst and images two.

Make the text inviting

Choose a typeface which is easy to read and try not to use more then two in any one publication. Use different sizes and the bold facility for variety. Also try to:

- ⊙ Avoid using CAPITAL letters for complete words to highlight important text because it makes it more difficult to read. Make your text stand out by increasing the size and/or **putting it in bold**.

- ⊙ Make the text easier and more inviting to read by not crowding it with other design features. Headlines also stand out more if there is sufficient white space around them.

- ⊙ Avoid using large blocks of text in italic as this can be difficult to read. A paragraph of italic is probably long enough.

- ⊙ Keep the text as big as possible. The body copy in this book is reproduced in 10 point and this is probably as small as you would want to go; anything smaller is very hard to read.

Variations in Helvetica point size and font weight

Roman: Abc 10pt Abc 12pt Abc 14pt Abc 16pt

Medium: Abc 10pt Abc 12pt Abc 14pt Abc 16pt

Bold: Abc 10pt Abc 12pt Abc 14pt Abc 16pt

Heavy: Abc 10pt Abc 12pt Abc 14pt Abc 16pt

Dealing with colour

When choosing colours make sure you think about how all the different elements in your design will work, eg, text is always best in a dark colour. It is also not advisable to reverse large blocks of text out of a dark colour as it can be very hard to read. If you have a background colour make sure that all images and text will be readable on top of it.

Selecting the best image

Select an image (photo, transparency, cartoon) that best communicates your message and has a good, focussed composition. For example you may have two similar photos of children in front of a factory. In one photo the children may be farther away and not looking at the camera. In the other they may be closer up and looking straight out of the picture which creates a different, more challenging mood. Decide which of these you feel will communicate your message best. Also try to:

- ⊙ Use people to put things into context.
- ⊙ Write captions for your images. People usually look at captions before reading a main block of text.

Consistency

Consistency will help strengthen people's awareness of both your group and your campaign. Here are some ways you can be consistent.

- ⊙ Make sure that you use your logo in the same way on all publications. Often a black and white version looks the most effective.

- Select fonts and colours and use them throughout all your publications.
- Devise a style in which to present your address/details and use the same style every time.

Printing your publications

To get a quote for a print job you will have to telephone the printer with details about:

- How many copies you want (and by when).
- What kind of paper you want to use. At Friends of the Earth's offices we specify 100 per cent post-consumer waste recycled paper.
- The size of the publication.
- How you would like it folded. (For example an A4 sized piece of paper could be folded in half once to make an A5 leaflet or in thirds, twice, to make a traditional leaflet (printers sometimes call this size DL or A4 folded to a third A4).
- How you plan to supply your design. Will it be a print out (hard copy) or will it be on a computer disk?
- How many images need to be scanned. All but the smallest images will probably have to be scanned by the printer.
- How many colours you want. The job will either be one colour (any colour of your choice); two colour (any two colours of your choice) or four colour (by using cyan, magenta, yellow and black inks you will be able to produce a full colour publication). Black is a colour, but the white of the paper does not count as a colour.

⊙ ⊙ ⊙ Top Tips ⊙ ⊙ ⊙

Test your design

Find out if your leaflet or poster is going to work well by trying it out on your audience before it is printed. Don't just check that there are no spelling mistakes or wrong phone numbers. Ask your tester if they can tell you what the key message is. You may find that your family's first impressions are very helpful.

3 Getting the message across: talks and presentations

There are going to be occasions when you will want to tell people about your campaign more formally, perhaps by a talk or presentation. Reasons for giving a talk include:

- ⊙ To urge other groups and organisations to support your campaign.
- ⊙ To persuade decision makers such as your local authority to implement what you want.
- ⊙ To let other organisations know about your work as part of a fundraising/recruitment drive.

Before you agree to do a talk think through the following questions:

- ⊙ How will it further the work of our group?
- ⊙ What will people do as a result of hearing me – join our campaign, join our group, sign our petition, give us money?
- ⊙ Am I the right person to give this talk?
- ⊙ Do I have the time to do it?

Know your audience. Are they potential allies or enemies?

Do not feel pressurised into doing something just because you are asked to do it. If it does not fit in with your campaign objectives, or if you are too busy — just say no.

If you do decide to go ahead with the talk, prepare by working out:

- ⊙ What exactly does the person who first asked me to talk, want me to talk about? Is the brief the same?
- ⊙ Who is the audience? Are they potential allies or enemies?
- ⊙ Am I giving a presentation or a debate? If it is a debate, who else is speaking?
- ⊙ How much time do I have for my talk?
- ⊙ What equipment will be available to help? You may need a slide projector, overhead projector or flipchart if you plan to use visual aids.

Prepare properly
Don't gamble on being alright on the night with a couple of pages of scribbled notes. Careful preparation will make your talk sound professional.

Decide on the objective of your presentation and which bits of information are crucial to include in your talk. Then structure your talk so that it has a:

- ⊙ **Beginning** Who I am, why me, I'm here to talk about..., because..., I'm going to talk for 20 mins... etc.
- ⊙ **Middle** Stick to three or four points (along the lines of what is the problem, what you can do, what we have done) as this is what most people will remember.
- ⊙ **End** Summarise the main points and finish on an upbeat call to action, eg, "If there is one thing I'd like you to remember/do after this evening it is..."

Practise
Write or type out your entire speech on paper and then rehearse it. On the day, do not read your speech as it will sound monotonous and will not grab people's attention. If necessary, write down the key points on cards and use these as a prompt during your talk. Go through your speech in your head, whenever you can. You do not have to know it off by heart but you should know the general outline. This will make your talk sound natural and interesting to listen to.

Practise in front of people (or even in front of a mirror). It may feel silly standing up in your front room, but it will make the real thing go much smoother. The advantage of saying your speech in front of people is that they will be able to pick up on any nervous habits, such as saying "um" or "you know". Once you are aware of habits like this they are much easier to control.

Humour can make the presentation more enjoyable. If it is an evening meeting people will have given up their free time to be there. You do not have to be a stand-up comic, but the odd flash of humour will warm people to you and your campaign.

⊙ ⊙ ⊙ Top Tips ⊙ ⊙ ⊙

Speech writing

⊙ Reinforce your points with a few facts. Do not overdo it and make sure they are accurate.

⊙ Think about what might appeal to your audience.

⊙ Always emphasise the benefits of what your group is doing.

⊙ Be positive. If you've had a success or something has gone well, say so.

⊙ Plan your speech so that people's feelings move along, eg, if you want to fire people up, make sure you leave them with hope and determination.

⊙ Avoid jargon unless you are certain that your audience will be familiar with it.

Before the talk

Check out the venue before you give your presentation. Arrive early so that you can familiarise yourself with the room and the equipment. Get a friend to sit at the back of the room and practise the start of your talk to check if you can be heard from the back of the room.

Visual aids

Use visual aids to focus the audience's attention and illustrate your points. Consider how you are going to use these. Which is the best medium – a flipchart, an overhead projector (OHP) or slides? They do not need to be fancy computer-produced materials but they do need to be easy to read/interpret. Do not have too many – one overhead transparency or slide per minute of your talk is ample.

Giving your talk

Remember the audience wants to hear a good presentation. They do not want to put you on trial. If you have prepared well then this should help calm your nerves. Everyone is human and likely to make mistakes – what may seem like glaring errors to you may be missed by the audience who does not know your presentation. Even if things go disastrously wrong the main thing to remember is that you are there to get a message across.

Do not talk to your overheads. Speak to the audience and especially the people at the back of the room. Speak more slowly and clearly than in everyday conversation. If people ask you to speak up, make sure that you do. It may feel like you are shouting but if the acoustics in the room are bad the people at the back will need all the help they can get.

⊙ ⊙ ⊙ Top Tips ⊙ ⊙ ⊙

Giving talks

Inject a personal note – tell a story (short!) about something that happened to you or relay your thoughts – even if it's just a quick aside. It makes you seem human and may warm people to your campaign.

Don't be fooled into thinking that you have to know everything. The best talks have a clear theme or message running through them. Make the most of being one of the 'people' and appeal to your audience.

Questions

Questions show that people are interested in what you have said. Remember that you are likely to know far more about the issue than they do. If people ask you tricky questions pause briefly and collect your thoughts before answering them. If you do not know the answer, do not be afraid to say so. Either pass them on to another person in the room who may know, or say that you will get back to the questioner with information when you have had a chance to find out. Do not go into intricate discussion on a minor detail with just one person in the audience. You can always say words to the effect of, "This is an interesting issue – maybe we can continue this discussion after the meeting?"

What else to take with you

Take campaign materials including any fliers, briefings, leaflets and membership forms. Remember to have collecting tins on the door, so that people can donate to your campaign. A sheet of paper for people to sign up for more information will be essential as people rush to join you after your rallying cry!

More about publicity   Part 4

Upping your PR game

1 Media basics

This is the age of the spin doctor. It can seem as if feeding information to journalists is a mysterious skill known only to a handful of highly trained initiates. But using the media successfully is possible if you follow some basic guidelines.

Getting your story into the media is one of the most important aspects of local campaigning. This is because widespread media coverage is by far the quickest, cheapest and most effective way to reach the people you want to hear your message. A local newspaper is read by thousands. A national news programme is watched by millions. Even the most committed person distributing leaflets cannot reach so many in so short a time. Media coverage can also raise the profile of your campaign and help put pressure on decision makers.

The media is shorthand for a wide variety of publishing formats. These include:

- ⊙ Newspapers   National dailies (tabloid and broadsheet) – national Sundays – regional dailies – local pay weeklies – local free sheets.

- ⊙ Magazines   Including trade press (such as *Water Bulletin, Construction News*) and a vast range of special interest publications (such as *Ethical Consumer, Tomorrow*).

- ⊙ Radio   National and local services.

- ⊙ TV   National news and current affairs – regional news and current affairs.

There are also news agencies for both national and regional stories. News agencies like the Press Association (PA) and Reuters write stories and send them on to newspapers and broadcasters. Much of what you read in your regional daily will be taken directly from the PA.

Media organisations have vastly different levels of staffing. The BBC nationally employs hundreds of journalists. Your local free sheet may have only one or two. But every media outlet, whether in print or broadcast, has to fill its space with stories. Your mission is to supply them. Find out which papers, radio and TV channels cover your local area. Check in your local newsagents and library to find out the names, contact details and interests of your region's media. Make up a list of media outlets, with names, telephone and fax numbers. Update it regularly.

Every media organisation works to deadlines. Find out what they are. Your local weekly paper may have to collate its news together by Wednesday night each week. If so, get the story there on Monday morning or even Friday the week before. Do not ring at 4pm on a Wednesday afternoon and expect a happy shout of, "Hold the front page!" For a daily paper, aim to make your press release arrive by lunch the day before publication, or even earlier if possible. For radio and TV, the same rules apply.

Know who they are
Find out the names of key journalists in your area. Find out what areas they cover – and if you can, their pet subjects. If you expect to deal with them regularly, suggest a drink after work or even lunch – personal contact is as important in the media as in any other business. If journalists know, like and trust you, your tip-offs and news stories are more likely to get coverage. Make sure that you can always be contacted for fact checking or to offer a short comment by providing a home and work number. To make sure opportunities for a soundbite are not missed you should also make use of an answer phone, mobile and/or pager. There is nothing more frustrating for a journalist than to be unable to contact key sources before deadline.

All news organisations have a "news desk" or equivalent. This is the central clearing point for press releases. If the news organisation is big enough, consider sending a copy of your press releases to the news desk as well as to a named journalist.

Know what they want
Journalists want news stories. It is not easy to describe what makes a good news story, but a key ingredient is something involving local people or local personalities. Other elements include controversy; previously unpublished facts (hence the number of items which include line such as, "A leaked Council report shows..." or "Shock new research reveals...") as well as visual appeal. What you find interesting, or important, is not necessarily news. Opinions are not usually news either. You can (and of course should) express an opinion, but only if you are also presenting news. External events often help make a good story.

Disapproving of plans to build a new road past your home may only become news if campaigners organise a demonstration of outraged homeowners, some dressed in costumes, at the meeting councillors are expected to vote for the plan.

Writing press releases

The media finds out about many stories from press releases so you need to know how to write them. Here are some simple rules to follow that will increase the chances of your press release being read by the news editor. See Useful tips, page 102 for a sample press release.

Use headed paper Make up a press release template, which you can copy and use again and again. Use the campaign logo (if you have one) and the name of your group in large writing at the top. Then the journalists will come to recognise your group. Put the words "Press release" in large type at the top.

Give key details Put the date and time of publication at the top. You can either mark a press release "For Immediate Release" which means it can be used immediately, or you can mark it "Embargoed until...(put specific date and time)", which means it cannot be used in advance. Do not embargo releases if you do not need to do so.

Think pictures If your press release advertises a demonstration or other visual event, put the words "Picture Opportunity" on it, and give a date, time, and clear address (with map if necessary) of the event.

Stay in touch Put full contact details at the bottom of each page with telephone numbers. If journalists can only reach you at specific times, say so. To stop extra pages from becoming lost, put the page number at the top of each page of your release, (eg, page 1 of 2).

Make it interesting Try to grab the News Editor's attention with a clever, appropriate headline. For example, "Mandelson's Birds in Sex Change Shock" was a story about gender disrupting chemicals in the Tees Estuary, part of MP Peter Mandelson's constituency, which attracted considerable coverage.

Put all the key facts in the first paragraph The first sentence of every news story tells you who, what, when and where. The rest of the story will expand these facts and try to answer the questions why and how. Use short sentences and clear English throughout. Avoid using jargon.

Include a quote Include a snappy quote from the key campaigner. Remember, the quote is reported as speech, not a footnote from a PhD thesis – so make it sound interesting. For example, if your group is disappointed at climate change discussions work out a snappy soundbite like: "These politicians care more about photo opportunities than global warming. The whole summit was about as green as a multi-storey car park" It will get more coverage than: "We are disappointed at the apparent lassitude which overcame world leaders when deliberating on the consequences of increased CO_2 emissions."

Add a section called "Notes to Editors" at the end, if you need to. This is for more detailed information, explanations about toxic chemicals, spelling out formula (such as CO_2) and acronyms, references and so on. Keep this section brief.

Keep the press release short Two sides of A4 in a fairly large typeface is really the maximum. Aim to use just a single side of A4.

Sending it out Distribution by fax is by far the best method. You may find it useful to fax straight from a PC, using a multifax programme. But if media outlets are close by you can always deliver your press releases by hand.

Know how to follow up

Your group's brilliant press release has been faxed to every newspaper, radio and TV station in Mytown. Now, you must follow it up. Ring key journalists (or news desks) to make sure they have received it, and find out if there is anything else they want to know. Yes, this will make you feel like a door to door toothbrush seller, but newsrooms are chaotic and sometimes press releases get lost. When the news desk says "No, never seen it before", they may even be telling the truth. Send it to them again.

If someone breaks an embargo, claims that you have said something which you have not, rewrites facts and figures or otherwise mistreats you, it is perfectly reasonable to complain. Be polite, but firm. Similarly if someone does a good article about your group's campaign, there is no harm in saying thank you.

2 Over the airwaves and on the box

Because your press release was brilliantly written, and because you are a local campaigner, you could be rung by dozens of TV and radio stations wanting an interview. At this point, many people start to panic. So take a deep breath, and follow these simple rules. Not everyone can be a TV genius, but anyone can do a decent job.

Don't panic. Make sure you have understood whether the interview is on location, via the telephone from your home, or in the studio. Check whether the interview is live, or recorded. Many interviews are pre-recorded. That means the station will talk to you in advance of their programme, and edit what you say down to a few sentences. This has advantages and disadvantages. It means that:

- ⊙ You can think about what you are going to say.
- ⊙ You can start again if you get it wrong.
- ⊙ But you cannot control which of your remarks they choose to use.

In a pre-recorded interview, make the same point in four or five different ways. How many times have you heard a politician say the same thing again and again and again, always in five second sentences? Most annoying to listen to live, but if the interview is edited it will still make sure that their point gets across. If you get into a muddle while you are talking, stop. Say sorry, and ask for the question to be repeated. Interviewers are used to this.

Some interviews are live. On radio, they can be done down the telephone or live in the studio. If you have time, go to the studio. Your voice will sound better, you will make better contact with the interviewer, and you will be more convincing to the audience.

Decide what you want to say, and say it

Work out what you intend to say in advance. Remember, interviews are not conversations. You do not have to answer the question directly. If you are asked: "Aren't you just a bunch of NIMBYs?" (Not In My Back Yard). Do not say, however tempting: "No we are not, you ridiculous little man". Instead use the question as a prompt to make your points. So you could say: "Well, Jeremy, I'm a Mytown parent, and I'm worried that this new road will mean my child won't be safe when she walks to school. Mytown is for people, not for Ferraris".

Use the sound bite Sound bites are sentences which may take 10 or 15 seconds to say. They are the words that make what you have to say memorable. Churchill was a master of the sound bite. Think of: "I have nothing to offer but blood, toil, tears and sweat". Think of the sheer number of words that pour from your radio every day. Can you remember a word that an interviewee said in the last news broadcast you heard?

Make it personal It is your town, your child and your family that matters. Be expert, by all means, but be passionate as well. Communicate feeling. Remember that being a "talking head" is like being an actor. Remember how angry you were when that wildlife site was destroyed, or when the bulldozers turned up to begin work on that new road. Now find the words, spoken calmly, to communicate your feeling to the audience.

Make time Turn up at the studio early. Ask the programme makers what they are going to ask you. Ask the interviewer what the first question will be. They will often tell you.

If you find you are in a debate with someone, do not panic. Make simple points, clearly and calmly. Make sure you can back them up with one killer fact, if challenged. Do not hesitate to disagree – politely – but do not lose your temper. Do not be sidetracked from the points you want to make. If you are interrupted politely ask the other side to keep quiet while you are speaking.

If you are on TV, your appearance matters. Wear a suit or smart outfit and brush your hair. Try to look calm and alert and speak in a normal voice, as if you are talking in a front room.

Remember, your appearance matters if you're on TV

If it does not work first time

These are the basics. The key to all successful media work is repetition. Keep at it, and journalists will soon be ringing you. Sometimes they will ring when you haven't sent them anything at all, just to ask you to comment on their story, or to see if you have something interesting coming up. Then you will know that you have them hooked.

Be helpful, be truthful and be precise. A good joke is worth a hundred statistics. Trouble making can be fun... The public would rather believe a local person, such as you, than the politician or corporate group you are challenging.

3 Running a great event

Why run a campaign event?

Events and actions can make a big contribution to the success of your campaign. You can hold an event for a variety of reasons: to communicate campaign messages or demands; to give people the opportunity to participate and so increase support for your group or your campaign; to increase pressure on a particular target; to draw attention to a campaign issue; to demonstrate numbers and to raise money. The better planned your group's event is, the more effective your campaign will be.

Whether you are planning an event involving big numbers, such as a demonstration, rally or public meeting, or an action or photo stunt where the primary objective is media coverage, the steps are the same. It is only the time frame and the numbers of people involved that will change. Keep your planning on course by knowing the answers to the following questions:

- ⊙ Why do we want to hold the event/action? What's the opportunity?
- ⊙ Who is doing it? Who are our potential allies and partners? Who do we want to influence? Who will come to it and who is going to do the work?
- ⊙ What kind of event do we want to run? Outdoor? Indoor? Site-based? A meeting? A demo? A high street action?
- ⊙ Where do we want to do it? Venue? Site?
- ⊙ When do we want to do it? Is it time critical? Is there an external agenda driving this? Is it weather dependent? Have we got time?
- ⊙ How much is it going to cost and where's the money going to come from?

Planning the event

What's the story? Design your action according to your resources. If you can only rely on four people to turn up, do not plan something dependent on large numbers. Think about what will make the local media want to cover the story. Does it have a strong news hook? Is it a timely issue that's already on the news agenda? Does it have strong local relevance? Does it have clear demands and an obvious target?

Creative actions Get your group together and spend 10 minutes coming up with ideas. Be creative. When you have lots of ideas test them against your checklist. It is important to avoid trying to communicate too many messages or making the action overly complicated. Think captions. Will it make a good picture without a two-page explanation? Think about branding. How will people know who you are? Think banners, placards, props, costumes.

Remember, if you want to influence the public directly, it is important not to be too confrontational. You are far more likely to get your message across if you make people think. Be entertaining, witty, challenging, creative, informative. Chanting or singing is OK, but abuse is not. You should never intimidate people. If you can involve kids or celebrities, all the better.

Tasks Recruit people to help. Look for people with theatrical flair who do not mind drawing attention to themselves. But also find people who are highly creative or practical as prop or costume makers, banner makers, ideas' merchants and photographers. Sort out tasks in advance. Agree who is going to stage manage the event; who is going to liaise with the media, the police and your target (eg, supermarket staff). Agree who is going to be media contact. Agree who is going to participate in your action, street theatre or whatever. Do not try and do everything yourself.

Locations Sometimes what seems like a good idea on paper falls down when you check the location. Think about sightlines, distance and perspective. Will there be room for a photographer or cameraman to get a good shot? Can a picture include you, your group, the action, your banner and the name or your target (a supermarket, garage, recognisable local landmark). Think about what it would look like on TV as well as the printed page, make it interactive rather than static. If you want to interact with the public, costumes can make actions more theatrical, less threatening and you can always take along fliers to hand out to ensure the public find out more about what you are doing.

Legal issues

Think about safety For example could your action pose a potential danger by making people walk into the road to avoid you? Avoid obstruction – blocking the pavement may prompt police involvement – so do not give them that excuse. The public has a right to pass and re-pass on a public highway – so as long as they can do that, you should be on the right side of the law.

Informing the police It is always worth informing the police if you are planning an action in a public place. If you are not breaking the law, there is no reason why you should not exercise the right to protest peacefully. But if requested by the landowner, store manager or whoever, you should take notice of the police if they ask you to move on.

Public processions If you are planning an action which involves a march or "public procession", you should provide six days' advance written notice with specified details (date, start time, route and organiser) to the police station in the area where the procession will start. In Northern Ireland an application form must be completed at least 28 days in advance of the planned march. You will need police co-operation for big events anyway and the police can be very helpful in directing traffic, or advising on good routes between different places, such as a station and rally site.

Trespass What about trespass – will you have time to set up your stunt or carry out your action before being asked to leave private premises? If your action is on private property, you should try and negotiate to do the action before moving on. If you leave when asked, it is unlikely the police will interfere. Being removed from a supermarket, for example, during a peaceful protest, can make good photographs.

 The laws regarding obstruction, trespass, breach of the peace are complex and these notes are for guidance only. In general, if you are planning a mass action, it is important to check out your legal position in more detail, according to the specifics of what you are planning. For more information see Useful reading on page 108.

Publicity

This is essential for your event to be a success. If you are publicising a meeting, rally or march try to put up fliers and posters in as many local outlets as possible. Leaflet near the site or on the high street. If you can afford it, book an advert in the local paper. Promote your event through all your own and other organisations' newsletters and literature and try and get a mention on local radio. If there are local celebrities supporting you, use them to publicise your event too.

If you have a good relationship with the media, try and get publicity about your event in advance. Bear in mind that it is easier to get journalists to attend an event held on a weekday rather than the weekend. If work responsibilities of your members make this difficult, try and hold the event early in the morning (eg, before 9am). This has the added bonus of the possibility of breakfast coverage on radio and TV stations, which often have high viewing/listening figures.

Mass events

Planning an external event with big numbers, such as a march or rally, will involve many of the same steps as planning a small action on the high street.

◉ ◉ ◉ Top Tips ◉ ◉ ◉

Mass events – planning checklist

Indoor events

Booking a venue for a public meeting or indoor rally

- ⊙ Check capacity, accessibility, cost.
- ⊙ Does venue have a PA system and any other audio visual equipment?
- ⊙ Is there room for stalls or exhibitions?
- ⊙ Catering arrangements?

Outdoor events

Choosing a site for a rally, march or walk

- ⊙ Check public access and rights of way.
- ⊙ Check if permission is needed from the landowner or council or Road Service in Northern Ireland. You should also contact any local people who might be inconvenienced.
- ⊙ Liaise with the police about access routes to and from site.

Mass events – planning checklist continued

- ⊙ Check the distance of the march/walk/rally, the kind of terrain to expect and advise as to suitable clothing and whether the event is suitable for children.

- ⊙ Check out the start and how to get there. You may need to organise transport to ferry participants to the site or start of the route, and car parking arrangements.

- ⊙ Consider the availability of public transport as you may need to arrange shuttle buses from town centre to site.

- ⊙ Check out the finish if route is not circular and ensure a map is available.

The route

- ⊙ Organise signage and route markers.

- ⊙ Organise refreshments and food concessions; water supply?

- ⊙ Check access to loos and whether you need to hire portaloos.

- ⊙ Hire staging and tent/marquee; or use a flatbed, open-sided truck; hire a PA system.

- ⊙ Consider whether you want to set up information stalls.

- ⊙ Ensure you have first aid provision. Contact Red Cross or St John's Ambulance.

- ⊙ Recruit stewards who should wear high visibility jackets, tabards or armbands. Identify a chief steward who will liaise with safety co-ordinator and event manager; prepare stewards' briefing.

- ⊙ Organise something for people to do, such as petition signing, postcards. Consider entertainment such as kite flying, face painting.

- ⊙ Organise recycling points and a litter-pick.

From the frontline

Leeds Friends of the Earth organised a range of events to stop peat extraction on Thorne and Hatfield Moors. "The campaign started by targeting gardeners, who are the main users of peat," explains Elli Groner of Leeds FOE. "Dressed as Bill and Ben the 'flower pot men', we visited garden centres to persuade people to buy peat free compost. A few months later we arranged a picnic in Thorne for gardeners in Leeds to show them the uniqueness of the site first-hand". The group also performed a street play in Thorne market one Saturday morning which received fantastic coverage, especially from the local media. People hearing about it on the radio, including several local councillors, then turned up to see the group in action.

The renewed support for the campaign in the local area then meant that another event a couple of months later was also a great success. A protest was organised on the moors with a 20ft banner which read "Bog off Scotts" – a witty, pithy slogan targeting Scotts, the company extracting the peat. *"Both local MPs joined us at this event, which was covered by the national press and we appeared on television and in* BBC Wildlife *magazine. It is a great feeling to see the local streets buzz, but we still have a way to go to save the moors,"* declares Elli, *"even if we have had a very good time organising all the actions."*

⊙ Tip Events can also benefit from having a unique prop which will interest the public and attract the media. The next section looks at how to make props for your events.

4 Props on a shoestring

A well chosen prop or costume can transform your event from a solitary table on the street into a crowd-gathering stunt.

You do not necessarily have to make a prop. Here are some tried and tested options:

Hire it Try the Yellow Pages under Fancy Dress or Theatrical Supplies. Costumes can cost anything in the range of £20 to £40 to hire, but it is worthwhile asking for a discount – they may be sympathetic to your cause.

Get someone else to make it Find some sympathetic (or publicity-craving) artists at your local art/sculpture/drama department or street theatre group. Or get a local school to build it as a project.

If you do build your own, then:

Simplify it Try and see the overall shape as simple geometrical units. Get the basic form, not the details. A chain saw is just a box and a flat rectangle. A tree is just a big tube and smaller tubes. Get lots of tubes and join them together. Then smooth over with papier-mâché (use PVA wood glue, not wallpaper paste).

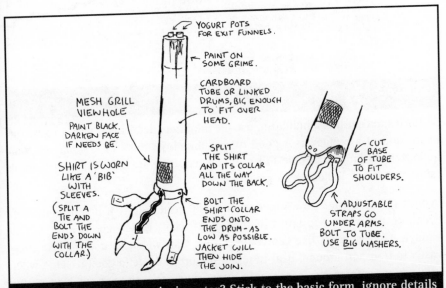

Trying to build your own incinerator? Stick to the basic form, ignore details

Stick to simple shapes. Then transform the basic shape with colourful paint. For example use bright yellow on your homemade bulldozer to make people think, "that's a JCB digger". Without paint, props tend to look amateur and scruffy.

View it from a distance Do not add details that will not be seen. Exaggerate the details, make them bold, not realistic. Better still, do not build 3-D details if you can just paint them on. Coloured papers are even quicker than painting.

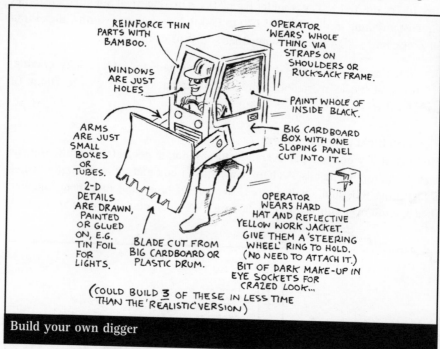

REINFORCE THIN PARTS WITH BAMBOO.

WINDOWS ARE JUST HOLES.

OPERATOR 'WEARS' WHOLE THING VIA STRAPS ON SHOULDERS OR RUCKSACK FRAME.

PAINT WHOLE OF INSIDE BLACK.

ARMS ARE JUST SMALL BOXES OR TUBES.

2-D DETAILS ARE DRAWN, PAINTED OR GLUED ON, E.G. TIN FOIL FOR LIGHTS.

BIG CARDBOARD BOX WITH ONE SLOPING PANEL CUT INTO IT.

BLADE CUT FROM BIG CARDBOARD OR PLASTIC DRUM.

OPERATOR WEARS HARD HAT AND REFLECTIVE YELLOW WORK JACKET. GIVE THEM A 'STEERING WHEEL' RING TO HOLD. (NO NEED TO ATTACH IT.) BIT OF DARK MAKE-UP IN EYE SOCKETS FOR CRAZED LOOK...

(COULD BUILD **3** OF THESE IN LESS TIME THAN THE 'REALISTIC' VERSION)

Build your own digger

So for instance if it is a bulldozer, use the minimum details you need to give the impression of a bulldozer. A good rule of thumb is: think of a simple cartoon bulldozer. As long as people think "bulldozer", you are OK, and if they think "silly pantomime bulldozer" – great!

What's the shelf life? How long does the prop need to last? If it is for a one-off event, do not make it to last a lifetime. Electricians gaffer tape is often strong enough. Use materials like cardboard, rather than wood, as it will make them easier to transport around. Bear in mind that props do get a good bashing when used, so re-enforce the cardboard – tape bamboo behind weak edges, and polystyrene blocks into corners. And does it need to be waterproof in case of rain?

Make it light A heavy prop is exhausting to wear and carry. Can it be built in pieces and dismantled for transport? Even a cardboard prop can be disassembled: use large bolts, big washers and wing nuts, and strengthen the bolt holes with taped-on plastic sheets cut from washing up liquid bottles.

Make it cheap Check your attic, car boot sales or jumble sales for good sources of free materials. Wood off-cuts can be useful.

Keep it simple Does the prop express a simple idea? Would it work as a photo in the paper? Emphasise the point with a clear slogan. Co-ordinate your leaflets/posters with the prop.

Keep it striking Would it make you look twice? Repetition is a good trick: three of the same thing will have more impact than one. Can you add music or sound effects? Do something unusual: stage a 'funeral' and label the coffin, eg, My Local Park, Our Local Shops, Our Lungs...

Keep it brief If there is a story, make sure it is told quickly – keeping the attention of an audience for a long story is difficult. What about recruiting some drama students?

Keep it funny Add a twist of humour. Satire puts your opponents in the killjoy role, and warms people to you.

Keep it big Outsize everyday objects are striking – build a giant chainsaw, or a giant test tube.

Keep it moving A prop that moves is better than a static one, so put someone inside it (rucksack frames make good mounts). Why stay put when you can tour the town? Pay a visit to the "lion's den" (the council, the supermarket you are targeting). If you are told to move on, do so.

Keep it versatile A giant can-of-worms will serve for several different issues – just change the label each time. Make it to look like a giant Jack-in-the-Box and then add something appropriate to your campaign, like, "More shopping centres!" "More traffic jams!"

◉ Tip Think about where you are going to store your prop. Props get ruined because no-one thinks about this in advance.

Keep trying

There's no better advice than experience. Can you guess which worked and which didn't? (Answers on page 76.)

1 **Alien visitors** Five silent, almond-eyed aliens (papier mâché heads built around big pear-shaped balloons, plastic colander eyes) exploring city centre consumerism and waste. Leaflets saying "People of Earth, we come in peace, but we do not understand why...(a,b,c.): please explain!"

2 **Major in a cage** John Major mask (joke/novelty shop) locked inside a cardboard prison on wheels, being dragged through town by a high court judge (costume hire). Big sign saying "**Guilty**".

3 **Stick of rock** Huge stick of rock labelled "Arms trade sweeteners". Used for a tug of war between military dictators and arms trade protesters.

4 **Third World see-saw** A long see-saw representing the scales of justice. Third World farmers at one end (dressed in simple ragged clothes) and at the other large blocks of concrete representing the cash crops they'd need to grow to earn a decent living. Narrator explains this, and asks, "How many will it take... One? Two?, etc.". In fact it takes lots of blocks, symbolising how the global trade system is stacked up against the poor.

5 Creating a website

The internet is rapidly becoming the most cost-effective method of getting your message across to the general public. Web publishing is as good as free because there are zero print and mailing costs. That is why even if the only function that your website performs is to advertise the time of meetings and the areas you campaign on, you might get lots of new members.

How do I get a website?

Web space is generally free for non-commercial use and if you have an existing e-mail account you should be offered web space. In order to get your pages on to the web you will need two things:

- ⊙ An account with an Internet Service Provider (ISP) to host your web pages. You can find lists of ISPs and a breakdown of their recent performances in Internet magazines and in *Which?*.

- ⊙ A modem for your computer to plug into the telephone network.

How do I make web pages?

Web pages are written in their own special language, HTML. Do not let this put you off however as most people pick up the basics quickly. You could try following an online tutorial or work from a book instead, ask in your local bookstore for their best-sellers. Once you have a website you can very quickly fill it with information on all your campaigns – most modern word processors have the ability to save text as HTML, which you can then link directly into your website.

Design

You will find lots of examples of bright backgrounds on the web and people often think that their use brightens up otherwise dull pages. However this may not be as easy to read as black text on a white background. Ultimately, the best way to learn how to do web pages is to have a go, make mistakes, get a peer review and then revise until you become one of the experts.

Before you start making your pages

Objectives Writing the HTML is really the last thing to be done. Before that there are many issues to decide upon. First of all, agree the objectives of the website. This sounds like a simple task, but it is vital to the success of the site to try and define these in a "SMART" fashion (Specific, Measurable, Achievable, Realistic and Time-specific). For example you could aim for the website to be visited by 1,000 people in the first six months, 20 per cent of whom are then inspired to make contact with the group, either by e-mail, phone or coming along to meetings.

Audience Define your audience and what exactly you want them to do. If you would like your audience to look at lots of different pages, and do several different things (for example order a publication, join a network) you need to decide which is the most important? With careful web design, it is possible to encourage people to visit the most important page/pages with a gentle textual nudge and a link, eg, "If you are finding this information useful, then consider giving us your support?" leading to a join page.

Structure and navigation The next stage is to agree on the main functions/areas of the website. This will allow you to decide what should go on your navigation bar. Check out other popular sites to see how they let you navigate. Hopefully, with good navigation any reader will be able to tell where they are in the site, how to get home, and most importantly, how to find the information they are looking for with the minimum number of clicks. Give people what they want to keep them happy and they come back.

Artwork/design Having agreed the above details, it is sensible to think about getting professional graphic design input. You may be lucky enough to know a designer, but otherwise, it may be worth asking at a local college or university to see if there are any students willing to help you, or even look up your local internet design companies to see if they fancy doing some voluntary work for you. Do not worry if you cannot find any budding designers. Just remember to keep things simple and concentrate on telling people what is going on locally – that is what they are interested in.

Regular site maintenance Work out who will do the updating of the site, which areas are likely to go out of date, and how often you are going to change your site. This is important as old information gives the impression of neglect and people will lose confidence in your site.

Marketing The final stage of any website policy is to define a marketing strategy. More often than not, websites are created at some effort and then no one looks at them because they are not aware of them. A marketing strategy is therefore really important. Things to think about are:

- Which organisations would you like to link to you?
- How visible is the site to certain search words, eg, "local, pollution, UK"?
- Have you submitted your pages to search engines?
- Do you want to collect the e-mail addresses of interested parties so that you can e-mail them when there are updates?
- Can you press release the site to local papers, or even get them to link to you?
- Are you in your local directories such as Yellow Pages, Scoot, Yahoo UK, and local government ones?

Web page design

- ⊙ Try to use capitals and bold sparingly, as you can only highlight so much, or you effectively highlight nothing.

- ⊙ Avoid using huge fonts on your page – it normally just takes up lots of space which could be used for something else.

- ⊙ Do not use the BLINK tag – it is very annoying.

- ⊙ Restrict the line width of the page using tables, so that the number of words to a line is no more than about 15. More words in a line can be difficult to read.

- ⊙ Spell check all your pages before putting them live. You would be surprised how often spelling errors creep into your web pages.

- ⊙ Give people a way to contact you with feedback about your site. This is an invaluable way of getting good suggestions as well as finding out things that do not work.

- ⊙ Think about using simple buttons and icons. They can really liven up your site. These can be simply designed using lots of free software readily available – explore one of the free software CDs that come with the internet magazines.

- ⊙ Try and keep each page short enough to fit into one browser window. Long scrolling pages are difficult to take in, so break them up into lots of linked smaller pages.

- ⊙ Try and keep the file size of your images to below 30 Kbytes for the whole page. This should allow your pages to load quickly.

From the frontline

Bristol Friends of the Earth set up its website in 1996. Before this the group was reliant on their bimonthly magazine to inform the general public about their campaigns.

"Bimonthly meant that the news was always old," remembers Julian Mellor, from Bristol FOE. *"The idea of the website was that it could contain up to the minute news of what was happening, and thereby build a much stronger network of activists and supporters."*

Initially the site did contain up to the minute news. When a local chemical plant blew up, the website was quickly updated to include details of the explosion, together with copies of letters from the local MP and links to the national pollution map. However due to questions over "ownership" of the site and difficulties of updating it, due to other commitments, the site became a snapshot of the year's campaigns rather than a profile of current action.

"So, before you start, think about how you communicate at the moment, think about what a website will add to your communications, think about who will run the site and think about how you will keep it constantly updated," advises Julian. *"Maybe it will just be an electronic leaflet, but being clear about what you are trying to do before you start avoids frustration and disappointment."*

Answers from page 72

1 People loved the aliens. It drew a huge crowd and lots of press.

2 The Major stunt was the best ever for the public. Simple and direct, but no press.

3 Poor. Too complicated. Some press, though.

4 Not one person stopped! It was hard work and short on humour.

Getting to grips with the system
Part 5

An insider's guide

1 Know your facts

At some point in any campaign you are going to need to delve deeper into issues in order to back up your position, demolish counter-arguments, or even uncover the whole truth lurking behind the opposition's version of a story. Sometimes the battle for a piece of information may turn into a campaign in itself, but stick with it and defend your right to know. If someone is keen to keep information confidential, there may well be a reason why they do not want you to find out.

If you need information about finding out who is on a council committee or want to look up statistics on drinking water quality, but do not know where to find it, ask people. Eventually you will come across someone keen to help.

Do not be afraid to ask for further explanation if you do not understand something. You may well come across jargon or technical details, and campaigners often need to grapple with legal issues. Nobody is expected to be an expert at everything, so keep on asking until you feel you have what you need.

Environmental Information Regulations

Aside from the law on local government information (covered in Influencing your local authority page 80), one of the most significant pieces of legislation is the Environmental Information Regulations (1992) and Environmental Information Regulations (Northern Ireland) 1993. This grants you access to environmental information held by public bodies, which includes bodies such as your local council, the Environment Agency, and in some instances privatised bodies with public responsibilities, such as the water companies. If you write a letter requesting some information, it is worth stating that the request is made "with reference to the Environmental Information Regulations". These regulations can be downloaded from Friends of the Earth's website at www.foe.co.uk/rtk/

You do not have to say why you want the information and you do not have to live nearby. Copies must be available at "reasonable" cost, and the information does not just have to be on paper. Disks of data and videos are also covered. The bad news is that there are some grey areas (for example, just what is environmental information), some loopholes and exemptions and charges for copies of information might be unreasonable, or too expensive.

Make sure that you get a full response to your request. If you are refused information, then ask under which part of the Regulations the information is denied. This will allow you to challenge the answer. Some of the grounds for refusal are optional, which means that a public body may withhold the information (but it may not). This means you can ask for a review of the decision or further justification. Other exceptions are compulsory, but you still might be able to challenge the interpretation. For example, information supplied voluntarily by a third party is subject to compulsory refusal. But you can still press further. Ask if the supplier has been asked if the information can be released – they may not actually mind.

Another key point is that the information should be supplied as soon as possible or within two months at the latest. This is sometimes interpreted as two months to reply, but you should press for a quicker response, particularly if the information is time-sensitive.

 The Environmental Information Regulations will be amended in the future, and may even be incorporated into the promised Freedom of Information Act. If you get into serious arguments over access to information, it would be worth checking that you have the latest version. Get hold of Friends of the Earth's fact sheet on access to information – see Useful reading on page 108.

Public registers

All sorts of information can be found in what are termed "public registers". These are essentially offices with information which has to be held by law. There are many different types of public register, ranging from a register of stray dogs to information on releases of genetically modified organisms, major industrial sites and water quality data. Many, but not all, registers are with your local council, the Environment Agency or the Scottish Environment Protection Agency. The Department of the Environment has a booklet describing public registers (see Useful reading on page 108). In Northern Ireland the Environment and Heritage Service at the DOE holds most public registers, so this should be your starting point.

General research

Here are some ideas for sources of information or help.

⊙ Libraries and librarians and newspaper archives, either at a library or at newspaper offices.

⊙ The internet – but pay particular attention to the source of the material. Is it from a respected body and can you be sure it is factual?

⊙ Lecturers at local colleges or universities.

⊙ Trade associations – often have statistics about their sector.

⊙ A consultant – you might be lucky to find one who can prepare a report relatively quickly for only a small amount of work, or you may find that a report has already been produced which gives you the sort of information that you seek.

⊙ Local council officers or councillors as well as your local elected representative and Member of European Parliament.

⊙ Do your own survey – even a straw poll of colleagues might be useful.

Contacting your adversary can also be a good idea. If you want to know how much money a company has spent on an Environmental Impact Assessment, compared with its advertising budget, why not write to the company – the answer may be invaluable. If the company does not give an answer, ask what it has to hide. If it does answer then you have some more facts at your disposal. If the company is rude or condescending to you, show their response to the press.

From the frontline

Infuriated at local council plans to cut recycling services in the city, Cardiff Friends of the Earth took to the streets to find out what the public thought. Working with a local expert in Social Science Research Methods the group designed and carried out a door-to-door survey of public attitudes to recycling in Cardiff. The survey found that 91 per cent of residents questioned felt that recycling was "quite important" or "very important" and that 71 per cent of residents believed that the changes proposed by the council would have an adverse effect on the level of recycling in the city. The final report was damning of the authority, particularly as Cardiff was declared "Recycling City" in 1990 but had only achieved a recycling rate of just 5.7 per cent. The evidence was used by councillors as well as the media and several of the proposed cutbacks were avoided.

2 Influencing your local authority

The world of local government is changing, with the start of political and economic devolution in England, Scotland, Wales and Northern Ireland. Many local authorities have now become unitary authorities, with responsibility for the provision of all services within a defined geographical area. This is true for Wales, Northern Ireland, the English metropolitan boroughs, the London boroughs, and some English shires, districts and cities. In the traditional English shires there is a two-tier county structure with the county council having responsibility for some services and the local district councils responsibility for others. For more information on recent changes in local government get hold of Friends of the Earth's fact sheet – see page 108 for details.

In Northern Ireland the local authorities have fewer responsibilities than local councils in England and Wales. See Friends of the Earth's fact sheet on campaigning in Northern Ireland (see Useful reading, page 108).

Detective work

The first step is to find out about your authority. Is it a unitary? Do you live in an English county that has recently changed, for example Berkshire is now six unitary authorities? Which district of your county do you live in and what are the relationships between the district and the county? For example, are they led by the same political party, or do they not see eye-to-eye on issues?

Information about your local authority can be found in your local library. In addition to the status of your authority, find out its contact details; what facilities it is responsible for; which department is located where and the various phone numbers of each department (your local phone book will have these details).

Local government information

Papers and background documents used in council meetings are available to the public. The law is the Local Government (Access to Information) Act 1985, and all council officials and councillors should be well aware of this. This gives you a right to attend council meetings, including those of any committees or sub-committees, except where some private affairs (like job applications) are under discussion. You will not normally be able to speak at council committee meetings though it is worth asking the clerk of the committee whether you can speak. You should be able to attend as an observer and have copies of the papers over which decisions are being made. These papers should be available three working days before the meeting. Article 23 of the Local Government Act (Northern Ireland) 1972 gives the public a right of access to district council, committee and subcommittee meetings in Northern Ireland.

Who is your council?

There are many ways of getting in touch, and influencing, your local authority.

Elected councillors Every local authority will have elected councillors who attend meetings and vote on policy decisions. This is where the political orientation of the council becomes important. Find out who the councillors are and which parties they represent. Also find out who is on which committee of the council and when each committee sits. The councillors may have regular surgeries and/or ward sub committees.

Officers As well as elected councillors, every local authority employs officers whose job is to do the day-to-day work of the council. There will be departments which report to the various committees (for example planning, environmental services, housing, education and social services). (These are not the responsibilities of local authorities in Northern Ireland.) Contact the enquires desk of the council to find out which officer is leading on a particular topic. The officers are public servants and should be pleased to hear from you, a resident who pays some of his or her wages. The council may also operate neighbourhood offices which act as a local drop-in centre for advice on council matters.

How it works

The local authority will be responsible for a number of decisions which you can influence, such as local transport, planning, education and health services. A sound knowledge of how the council works, the key officers involved in writing the reports on which councillors will vote, and names of the councillors on the various committees will help you in this task. If your group is able to mobilise members of your local community, by having good links with other groups in your locality, it can help you to influence the way decisions are made.

As well as knowing how they work, you should know what they say. Local authorities produce their own reports on nature conservation, transport, natural heritage in Mytown, as well as a Local Plan (which should be the planning blueprint for the locality for the foreseeable future). The next section explains how the planning system – including Local Plans – works in more detail.

How you can influence decisions

The power of the pen is not to be underestimated. Lobby your local council/relevant committee with letters from people supporting your campaign. You could aim for a story in your local evening paper, which may lead to local radio and TV coverage, forcing the council to defend or explain why such and such is going on. Sometimes issues even grab the attention of the national press, which could result in political embarrassment for a local leader with the national political party of which he or she is a member.

All of this activity will combine to make it very difficult for the local authority to take a decision behind closed doors and away from public scrutiny. You may also like to contact outside agencies such as the Environment Agency or your regional Government Office to seek their views on a particular issue.

It is vital to get to know how your local authority works and get it to work for you. And do not forget that while you can influence from within, it is as important to build and maintain your influence through keeping the pressure on by, for example, mobilising people and keeping the issue in the public eye through media coverage.

From the frontline

A Leicester campaign group enquired about the possibility of banning genetically modified (GM) foods in school meals at the education committee in March 1998. First they carried out a street poll in the city centre encouraging parents to write to councillors. The results were sent to the leader of Leicester Council, asking for the removal of GM foods from school menus. The campaign group then issued press releases, gaining press coverage. Letters were sent to all the members of the education committee with arguments about health and environmental safety, and asking for a policy review at the next meeting. At this meeting the question of safety was again raised and the committee agreed to investigate. The local paper picked up on this with a front page story and supportive leader column. Two days before a policy decision, a school gate poll was organised, with 91 per cent opposition shown to GM food in school meals. On 1 February 1999, the education committee made the decision to ban GM food from the city's school meals.

3 Using the planning system

Knowing how to use the land use planning system will help win campaigns. Campaigns to limit out-of-town shopping, encourage urban regeneration, reduce waste, control minerals extraction, create affordable local housing, arrange excellent public transport and protection of open and green space all hinge on the planning system. More and more local campaigning groups are using the system, realising that, like it or not, understand it or not, this is the way to have a say in what happens in your home area. To be successful you do not have to be an expert to use it. This section covers the basics of the planning system – for more information see Useful reading, page 108. Some organisations, such as Planning Aid, have trained volunteers which provide an advisory service for individuals and groups on planning-related issues – their contact details are listed on page 107.

Knowing how to stop offensive developments will be crucial to your campaign

What is planning for?

Land use planning is the system for promoting and controlling changes "in the public interest" to buildings and land use. It is supposed to ensure a "sensible pattern of development" and proper facilities to meet people's needs, such as housing, shops, open space and employment. It is not the task of planning to:

- ⊙ Protect the private interests of one person or group against the activities of another.
- ⊙ Intervene with competition between users of land.
- ⊙ Deal with issues that are subject to other laws, eg, noise, disturbance, litter.

Objections to planning proposals must always be made and justified on planning grounds. Devaluation of property and inconvenience of works for example, are not planning grounds for stopping a development.

A game of two halves

All councils, except in Northern Ireland (see Useful reading page 109 for more information on the planning system in Northern Ireland), have a legal duty to control development in their areas. They do this in two ways: development control and development planning.

Development control This is the 'reactive' half of planning, where councils receive and decide on planning applications. Most developments require planning permission, especially in conservation zones or where listed buildings are involved. Some minor works do not; such "permitted development" includes some house alterations.

Development planning This is the 'pro-active' half of the system, where councils draw up a development plan containing plans and polices for the use of land in their area. Councils will assess planning applications against their development plan as well as central government laws and advice – usually set down in Planning Policy Guidance (PPG), Regional Planning Guidance (RPG) and, in the shire counties, the County Structure Plan. In Wales, Technical Advice Notes (TANs) replace PPGs (the planning system in Wales is changing – see Useful reading on page 108 for more information on campaigning in Wales).

Local development plans

By law, councils will have a presumption in favour of any proposal that fits with their local development plan. A local plan sets out your council's preferred options and policies for use of specific sites. For example, derelict land may be earmarked for housing. So it makes sense to influence the plan before and while it is being drawn up. Trying to oppose a new superstore will be tougher if your local plan says that such proposals would be allowed on a particular piece of land.

Local plans are a long-term view – prepared about every 10 years with a mid-term review. They usually contain a map and a set of polices about how the area will be developed (or not as the case may be). Your local plan will cover broad policy areas such as housing, transport, shopping, open space, employment, the economy, water, buildings, tourism, nature conservation and sustainability.

As well as fitting in with national legislation and Planning Policy Guidance (PPGs), your local plan must fit with Regional Planning Guidance (RPG) and, if you are in a shire county, the County Structure Plan. So it is worth being sure about what these documents say or how they are being revised.

A public process

Drawing up local plans is a public process, though in practice few people participate apart from interest groups. It can take several years to gain full council approval. Unless no one objects to the proposed plan, there will be a local inquiry with a central government inspector appointed to decide any disagreements between the council and other parties. The inspector will recommend changes that the council will usually, but is not obliged to, adopt.

Who is involved?

Planning officers are the main players, as they deal with both halves of the planning process. In assessing planning applications, officers may visit the intended site and consult other council departments (a chance to use your influence). They may negotiate with the applicant and ask for a proposal to be amended to make it fit with the development plan. Officers will then write a report for the planning committee making the final decisions.

Councillors on planning committees usually follow officers' recommendations – but not always. They may propose amendments and ask for a decision to be deferred. Often, councillors give officers "delegated powers" to decide planning applications. So all in all, it is worth being on reasonable terms with your planning officers.

If an application is approved, planning conditions may be set. For example, the type of materials to be used, protection of open space and hours of operation. If the applicant appeals to the Secretary of State (the Department of the Environment, Transport and the Regions) against conditions or outright refusal of permission, a public inquiry will be held. Final decisions over planning applications are not formal until a decision notice has been sent. So the time to influence planning applications is before it goes to the planning committee stage.

⊙ ⊙ ⊙ Top Tips ⊙ ⊙ ⊙

Using your influence

Development plans

⊙ Try to get in early.

⊙ Meet relevant planning officers to discuss the general direction of the plan.

⊙ Make contact with key officers in other council departments to get their insight/support.

⊙ Give officers some key policies you wish to see in the plan.

⊙ Find out what other potential allies and opponents are doing.

⊙ Decide where your best efforts lie, ie, what section of the plan to focus on, eg, transport, economy.

⊙ Plan your submission carefully, based on planning grounds, using PPGs, RPGs and TANs to support, as well as object to, policies.

⊙ Produce an alternatives report.

Planning applications

⊙ Try to get in early.

⊙ Keep an eye on public notices in your local papers.

⊙ Get on the circulation list of relevant council committee papers.

⊙ Try to influence land use policy and planning proposals before they reach application stage.

⊙ Try to convince the applicant to improve their proposal.

⊙ If you still need to object, put your points in writing and ask for an extension to the normal time period (14-21 days).

⊙ When objecting, use planning grounds. Avoid petitions – written objections carry more weight.

From the frontline

In Autumn 1993 Islandmagee and District Conservation Society (IDCS) and Larne and District Friends of the Earth heard a rumour that Blue Circle was planning to use Magheramorne Quarry as a landfill site. This proposal threatened Larne Lough, which is a Ramsar site and a Special Protected Area, and would breach three European Directives (Birds, Habitats and Groundwater) if allowed to go ahead. In December 1994 a planning application for the landfill site was lodged. A letter writing campaign was started to object to the planning application. In all, 2,500 letters of objection were received by the planning department, and meant that the issue went to a public inquiry.

The public inquiry ran from 30 April 1996 to 12 June 1996. Larne and District FOE and IDCS split the job load and took seven topics each to respond to in the public inquiry. Finally the local campaigners won, after it was discovered that the tip would threaten an important colony of Roseate terns. *"This victory demonstrates that ordinary people can take on big business and win. Also remember that while a campaign is going on, any delays to the go ahead will be advantageous since policy or law may change in the meantime affecting the outcome,"* said Sharon Morrow one of the local campaigners.

4 Using the law

The legal system is roughly divided in two: criminal and civil. Both are relevant to environmental campaigns. The criminal system is for prosecutions in the magistrates court or the Crown Court; the civil system for compensation claims, injunctions in the county court or High Court, with the High Court additionally conducting judicial reviews of public decisions.

Before embarking on any legal action, decide whether it is worthwhile. Litigation can be expensive and in most cases victory is far from certain. It can also be time-consuming and can use up resources which may be better employed elsewhere. If you decide that the best course of action is a court order to stop something happening, an injunction, what do you do next?

Move quickly

There are likely to be three things against you, in addition to the law's innate preference for property rights over environmental rights. They are time, cost and restricted resources. Legal procedures are riven with time limits ranging from days to years. Furthermore, in a judicial review (see below) applying by its three-month deadline is not enough. You must apply promptly or risk having your application struck out.

Minimise your costs

Find a friend The cost of going to court can be enormous. But you can minimise it by preparing your case yourself or by getting a friendly lawyer to do it for you, possibly on a "no win no fee" basis. A number of affordable lawyers are used regularly by environmental campaigns – ask around for a recommendation. Alternatively, contact the Environmental Law Foundation (see page 106), which can put you in touch with a local member of their network.

You may qualify for legal aid The general practice of the Legal Aid Board is not to fund environmental cases (this may change with reform of the legal aid system). If you do get legal aid you will have all your costs and court fees paid for you (possibly subject to a monthly contribution). More importantly, you will be protected against the biggest hazard in going to court – having to pay the other side's costs.

Be prepared for costs Losing and having to pay the other side's costs can be devastating. A single hearing can cost as much as £20,000. Every subsequent hearing or appeal may rack the bill up even more. In some judicial reviews it is possible to get a pre-emptive costs order, whereby each side covers their own costs. But merely applying for such an order exposes the litigant to a costs order. It is vital for anyone going to court to have some sort of costs protection, especially if they have assets. An alternative to legal aid is insurance. However, like the Legal Aid Board, insurers are reluctant to support anything out of the ordinary. Consequently, in most cases the only viable costs protection is a fighting fund, supported by the community and/or a benefactor.

Putting a case together

Research the law To fight your case, you or your lawyer will need to research the law and gather evidence, all probably on a fixed budget. You should get hold of one of the many environmental law textbooks which are available now. But beware, they are of variable accessibility and will inevitably be somewhat out of date. There is no substitute for the raw law itself, probably best researched in the loose-leaf legal encyclopaedias kept at principal public libraries, such as Sweet & Maxwell's *Encyclopaedia of Environmental Law* or *Encyclopaedia of Planning Law and Practice*.

Research the internet Additionally, information can be gained via the internet. Court Rules can be obtained from the Lord Chancellor's Department's site, while Parliament and the European Commission similarly publish useful material. Some law firms now also provide free advice over the internet.

Use your right to know In assessing your case, you are likely to find that you need more information from a public authority. A vital tool in such a case is freedom of information legislation. These regulations, implementing an EU directive on the issue, provide everybody with the right to extract information relating to the environment from public bodies with responsibility for the environment, subject of course to certain exemptions. A public body must answer promptly on request and, within two months, provide the information sought or a reason as to why no disclosure is being made. The current legislation is shortly to be succeeded by a new Freedom of Information Act, providing a specific appeal mechanism as opposed to a judicial review as at present.

Keep good records All evidence relevant to your case must be carefully collected, recorded and preserved. Evidence can take the form of statements of eye-witnesses or experts. Or it can include photographs, video samples, diaries, letters, notes of phone calls, and public register entries. Such evidence must be uncorrupted and linked by sworn testimony to the events in question. If it can be corroborated, so much the better. Start collecting it now, making sure that all relevant dates and the names are recorded.

Two of the most effective ways in which environmentally harmful practices can be stopped are through criminal prosecution and judicial review.

Criminal prosecutions

A prosecution will be appropriate where an offence has been committed, for example a regulatory pollution limit has been breached or a statutory nuisance abatement order ignored. In the absence of a designated prosecutor in the relevant legislation, anyone can bring a prosecution by what is called 'laying an information". This is really not much more than a letter outlining the facts and the relevant law, with their local magistrates court. If the court is satisfied that a prosecution is justified it will issue a summons for the defendant to attend court and stand trial. It is then for you as the prosecutor to persuade the court that in the light of the evidence and the law, the defendant is guilty as charged "beyond reasonable doubt".

Judicial reviews

In essence a judicial review is very similar to a prosecution, in that it only proceeds on the permission of the court. A judicial review is a process whereby a decision by a public body is reviewed by a High Court judge to ensure that it has been made properly. Whether a decision in question is the right decision is not strictly speaking the concern of the judge, merely that it has been made according to the law.

Anybody may apply for permission for a judicial review, although they must be deemed by the court to have sufficient interest in the matter. In seeking permission the applicant presents legal grounds for the application supported by an affidavit on the facts in support. This can be done either at an oral hearing or on the papers (a "table application", which carries less initial risk in terms of costs). If the Court is persuaded there is an arguable case, permission is granted and a hearing is held at which the Court considers the full arguments of both sides. A more straightforward procedure exists for some planning matters.

With both procedures timing is extremely important. The requirement of promptness for judicial review applications has already been stated. Prosecutions of less serious summary offences must be commenced within six months of the offence itself. More serious indictable offences subject to a hearing in the Crown Court are not subject to this time limit.

Have the law, the facts and people on your side

Finally, in seeking to use the law, whether it be a prosecution or judicial review, it is useful to bear in mind the fact that effectively what you are doing is recruiting a judge or magistrate to your campaign. It is the judge who will or will not stop the bulldozers, and no amount of smart law work will count unless the judge is persuaded that not only the law supports your campaign, but that it is also worth their time and reputation intervening.

The efficacy of both judicial review (as a discretionary remedy) and criminal prosecutions relies on the gravity with which a judge or magistrate views a case. It is not enough simply to win the legal argument. You must impress on them that the case matters.

From the frontline

When Arthur Sedgely read that his local recreation ground, an area of historical and environmental importance, was being threatened by development, he was alarmed. Having consulted his local Citizens Advice Bureau he was referred to the Environmental Law Foundation (ELF). The first thing ELF did was discuss with Arthur how they could talk to other people in his area and see how they felt about the new development and then form a local community group. ELF then put him in touch with a team of ELF members – a solicitor, a barrister and a planning consultant who could provide legal and technical assistance. They were able to give the group advice and offer them a number of choices by which they could get involved in the planning process and stop the development. Planning permission for the development was refused. The developers have decided to appeal and ELF are continuing to provide advice to Arthur and the group.

5 Lobbying your elected representative

Elected representatives are MPs, members of the Scottish Parliament, Welsh Assembly Members, Members of the Legislative Assembly in Northern Ireland and MEPs.

Know who to lobby

Before you approach your elected representative there are several things that would be good to find out. The more familiar you are with their interests and background the more likely you are to be able to pitch your case in the most effective way. Find out his/her name, political party, occupation or background and address. Also find out the constituency boundaries (you can find this out from the local library), his/her surgery times and his/her interests – both financial and in terms of issues.

Lobby your elected representative

Why lobby your elected representative?

Lobbying is used to get a decision maker on board to give support for your case. Lobbying is best carried out at the elected representative's local surgery. If you are trying to interest your elected representative in a particular local problem, take him/her to look at it. If they are prepared to give you active support for your campaign they can help you locally by:

- ⊙ Making a statement supporting your campaign.
- ⊙ Using their influence with the local authority.
- ⊙ Speaking at public meetings.

Your elected representative should respond to your requests, and listen to your concerns. Your elected representative must explain their views on issues which matter to you. If they fail to do so, keep on at them. If your elected representative tells you that they do not support you, the next route is to try and change their mind. Two things will help you achieve this.

Good arguments in your favour Bringing new reports to the attention of your elected representative, sending copies of research papers, questioning him/her closely to ensure he/she has read the reports and meeting up with him/her to put the case – all these are useful ways to change his/her mind.

People power Even if you have irrefutable proof that your campaign should be supported, if you and your elected representative are the only two people who know about it, you may find your elected representative refusing to change his/her mind. If hundreds of other people also start to raise these points, then things may move your way rather more quickly. Try to persuade individuals and local groups, even the local media to lobby your elected representative too.

You can also bring people on board by asking them to sign an open letter to your elected representative. You can use pre-printed postcards, though these are far less effective than individually written letters. Handing out leaflets explaining your elected representative's position can also be effective – even if people do not actually write, your elected representative will be very concerned that so many people are finding out that he/she is not prepared to support a campaign to protect local wildlife sites, or stop the closure of a local service. A particular way of pressurising unsupportive elected representatives is to ask members of his/her own political party to lobby them, for example councillors (a list is available from your town hall), party officials (addresses in *Yellow Pages* under political organisations) and so on.

The power of the local media

Most elected representatives are far more concerned about their local media coverage than about their occasional appearances in the national press. They work hard at maintaining a high profile in their local media. They read local papers avidly, as they have to be on top of local disputes and events. So if you generate a series of letters in the local paper, or there are a number of reports on related problems – combined with good coverage of the possible solutions and a comment that your elected representative is not backing them – you may find the elected representative begins to shift his or her position. Never underestimate just how influential local papers are. Make good use of them.

Other routes to apply pressure

Ask parliamentary questions Elected representatives can ask ministers oral and written questions in parliament and the assemblies. As well as sometimes extracting useful information, this helps raise the profile of an issue. If you ask your elected representative to put down a particular question for you, be specific about the issue and the question. Ministers are more likely to give a specific statistic on a road-building programme than say why they support a particular scheme, although you can add at the end of your question, "and if [the minister] will make a statement" to elicit a more general position. Ask your elected representative to put down a written question, as the oral questions are drawn in a ballot – meaning you may wait months before your elected representatives gets lucky.

Writing to ministers If you think it is important that an issue is raised with the appropriate minister, you could ask your elected representatives to take it up with him/her. This guarantees a reply signed (and therefore seen) by the minister, whereas a letter direct from you to the minister is more likely to be answered by a civil servant.

Meeting the minister This may be useful, perhaps in combination with other local elected representatives affected by the same problem. Additionally, the elected representative can organise a delegation from a local community group to meet the minister concerned.

Adjournment debates This is a debate with the relevant minister instigated by an elected representative. These are drawn out of a hat, but it usually takes no more than a few weeks at most before an elected representative is chosen. Most of those on local issues last half an hour, although longer adjournment debates are available. The elected representative speaks first, followed by the relevant minister. If you persuade your elected representative to hold an Adjournment Debate, suggest that a summary of what he/she intends to say is sent to the minister in advance. This makes it more likely that the minister will be briefed on the points the elected representative plans to raise.

⦿⦿⦿ Top Tips ⦿⦿⦿

Useful parliamentary terms

Adjournment debate
A debate initiated by a backbench MP in which he/she gets a chance to debate an issue with the relevant minister.

Bill
A Bill is a proposal for law, which must pass several stages before becoming law, whereupon it becomes an Act. Private Member's Bills are introduced by a single MP rather than by the Government.

Early Day Motion
A House of Commons resolution to which MPs can add their names to demonstrate support for the sentiments it expresses. Among other things, this gives a list of supportive MPs and shows the support a particular measure has.

Green Paper
A Consultation document asking for responses on particular policy area. After the consultation period the Government will pull together the results and draw up its policy – published in a White Paper.

PPS
A Parliamentary Private Secretary is an unpaid assistant to a minister.

White Paper
Document setting out Government policy on an issue. Often followed by legislation to enact the policy.

Useful tips   **Part 6**

1 Making meetings work well – an outline agenda

7.30 pm Arrivals – display outline agenda

7.45 pm Prompt start/Introductions Try asking people to 'sign in' on a large sheet and say one thing about what they do in the group or what they are interested in (you can skip this if no one new turns up).

7.50 pm Agree draft agenda (displayed for everyone to see) Ask people if they are happy with the order of business and if any key or urgent issues are missing. Ask for Any Other Business (AOBs) items and add to end.

7.55 pm Best/worst thing What has happened since we last met? Bring up key business in a way that allows the group to review what worked and what could have worked better and to make sure nothing gets overlooked. Take notes to include in your next newsletter. (15 mins max)

8.10 pm Split into task groups So you can work on key issues, such as a campaign, planning an event or fundraising. Issues arising or actions needed can be written up on a large sheet for display during the tea break (about 20 mins).

8.30 pm Break/free time Any notices of other events could be displayed at a single point and people asked to look at them / sign petitions / sign up to events here.

8.45 pm Report back From task groups or individual campaigners (five mins each).

9.00 pm Forward planning This is where priorities and events can be considered from the ideas which emerged from the task groups or individual campaigners (30 mins).

9.30 pm Round up of action points Reminder of next events. Any other business (AOB) (15 mins).

9.45 pm Social time/drink.

2 Legal and constitutional issues

Any campaign group should have a simple set of basic rules, because once it needs to raise money or employ staff, or own property, then it takes on legal and managerial responsibilities. Your constitution should define who meets these obligations.

You are not legally bound to register your constitution, but if you do not you are an unregistered association. This means your campaign group has no identity of its own and individuals have to be nominated to act on behalf of the group to hold property or deal with finances. The good side is that you are less constrained by law and can more easily be wound up. The downside is that individuals can be held personally responsible for the group's obligations and debts, and individuals could find themselves sued for something that was not directly their fault.

To avoid this, the campaign group can become a limited company. It would then have to have a legal identity and could, for example, be sued and sue and own property. However it would have to obey rules set out by the Companies Act and submit details to the Register of Companies. A group constitution would have to satisfy the Companies Act.

You may qualify for charitable status – though there are rules on what you can and cannot do if you want to both campaign and have charitable status. The Charity Commission seeks to preserve the integrity of a charity and produces a range of leaflets – see page 105 for further details.

A Model Constitution

December 2000

Name and objectives

1 The name of the group shall be...

2 The aims of the group are...

Membership

3 Membership of the group is open to any person supporting the aims of the group, who pays a subscription fee as shall be determined by the Annual General Meeting of the group.

4 Membership is open to all persons without discrimination.

5 Only group members can participate in the election of postholders to the group and vote at the Annual General Meeting of the group.

Meetings and officers

6 The group shall have at least six meetings a year; to be known as General Meetings. Members shall be notified of all General Meetings at least ... days in advance. A General Meeting shall be the forum at which the major policies of the group shall be agreed. A record of all decisions taken at meetings shall be kept.

7 A General Meeting shall have a quorum to be determined by the Annual General Meeting of the group. If that quorum is not met, major group policy cannot be altered or formulated, nor can any expenditure above a sum to be determined by the Annual General Meeting of the group be sanctioned.

8 The group shall have a number of elected postholders (one of whom shall be a Treasurer). The duties of these postholders will include; managing the finances of the group and keeping accounts; distributing information to the appropriate postholders within the group. The minimum age at which people can act as postholders of the group is 16.

continued overleaf

9 The Treasurer shall be responsible for presenting the accounts of the group at least once a year to a General Meeting, and also to any other meeting if requested to do so by a General Meeting, at one month's notice.

10 The group shall open a bank or building society account in the name specified above. At least two of the elected postholders shall be signatories to the account, and at least two signatures shall be required on any cheque drawn on this account.

11 Policy decisions on a specific issue may be delegated at a General Meeting to a sub-group. The sub-group shall be required to keep records of its business and to report regularly at General Meetings.

12 The group must hold an AGM every year and re-elect postholders every year.

Resignations and termination of membership of the group
13. If any postholder wishes to resign (s)he shall inform the General Meeting in writing and/or verbally. When necessary a group member can be co-opted to carry out that postholder's duties until the next General Meeting. Election of a new postholder may take place at the following General Meeting.

14 The group has the right and responsibility to suspend or expel a member who has brought the name of the local group into disrepute, or been deemed to work against the aims of the group. Such a decision can only be made at a quorate meeting of the group, after at least one month's notice has been given to all members.

Termination
15 The group shall be wound up by a vote at an Annual General Meeting or by an Extraordinary General Meeting called for that purpose. Notice of intention to wind up the group must be sent to all members at least one month before any such meeting. At the meeting where it is decided to wind up the group, a decision shall also be taken as to what shall be done with any remaining funds.

3 Planning a local campaign

The following is an example of how a campaign works in practice. The campaign plan is by a local community group wanting to make it safer for their children to walk to school.

Campaign aim To make it safer for the local children to get to school.

Your objectives

1 Get a pedestrian crossing on the road in front of the local school.

2 Encourage fewer parents to drive their children to school.

3 School to give street awareness training to children.

Your targets

1 Local council: local councillor.

2 Local parents: parents of the children at the school.

3 Local school: school governors, children at the school, head teacher and teachers, parent teacher association (PTA).

Your key messages

1 Our children have the right to walk to school safely.

2 By driving your child to school you are putting your child's friends at risk.

Allies

1 Local councillor

2 Other parents

3 Teachers

4 Community police officer

Fact finding

1 Number of parents who drive their children to work.

2 Number of accidents on the road in the past 10 years involving children.

3 Which parents are on the PTA and who are the school governors?

4 Number of asthma sufferers in area compared to national average.

Tactics/actions to use

1 Poll of how many children already walk to school.

2 Lobby the local council – letters and petition.

3 Get local MP on side.

4 Encourage parents to write letters to the school asking for street awareness training.

5 Encourage the school governors to write in support of your campaign to the local council.

6 Poster competition in the school to help inform the children and their parents about street awareness.

7 Stunt – make own pedestrian crossing to use one morning.

8 Challenge chair of education/highways committee from the local council to walk to school one day with the children.

Campaign opportunities

1 Lots of public awareness that traffic has increased on the road.

2 They have just had to get a lollipop person for the road right in front of the school.

3 Local councillors' children are at the school too.

Media opportunities

1 Letters in the local paper.

2 Stunts and photo opportunities.

3 Encourage the local media to sponsor/support the poster competition.

4 Press release of events such as local MP giving their support.

Scheduling

Events which will make up your campaign calendar.

September

Initial research – poll of parents.

Letter to local councillor with the campaigns concerns.

Find out which parents are on the PTA and governors – ask to speak to them about the issue of the children's safety.

October

Organise a meeting with the local councillor and other concerned parents.

Write to the school with the results of the poll asking for them to take action and give their support to the campaign.

November

And so on...

Monitor the campaign

1 The amount of local press coverage.

2 The number of parents and teachers that show support for the campaign.

Evaluate the campaign

1 Publicly gaining support of the local MP.

2 If we manage to encourage the council to look into a new pedestrian crossing/safe routes to school programme.

3 Fewer parents driving their children to school.

4 Press release – a sample format

⊙ Use A4 paper.

⊙ Use a large, clear typeface.

⊙ Use simple words (avoid jargon).

⊙ Keep it short. One page is best, two pages is OK, three pages is too long.

⊙ When you have finished writing the press release double check that it is clear who did what, where, when and why and that contact details are correct.

Most press releases are organised in the same way, as you can see opposite. To make your group look professional include the following details:

⊙ Spell out who you are.

⊙ Your logo or group name.

⊙ Label it.

⊙ You need the words "Press release" "Media" or "News" at the top.

⊙ Number the pages.

⊙ Putting "page x of y" enables the news desk to see if they are missing part of the press release.

Timing matters
State if the press release is for "Immediate release" or put "Embargo until ..." and then add a date (and time if appropriate).

Now explain what is going on
Headline – think up a short, active headline (witty if possible).

Text – two paragraphs answering who did what, where, when and why.

Get a quote – include a snappy quote in spoken, not written English, from a key campaigner.

Make yourself available
Contact details – give a named person and all their contact details (including numbers at home, work, mobile and pager). Check that the contacts can in fact be contacted.

For immediate release: Monday 7 June 1999   page 1 of 1

GM Farmer rips it up!
Captain Barker gives GM trial the bullet

The first farm-scale GM trial site to be planted in the UK has been destroyed by the farm owner, it was revealed today. Captain Fred Barker, of Lushill Farm, Hannington near Swindon, ordered the destruction of 25 acres of GM oilseed rape over the weekend following objections to the GM crop from the farm trustees.

The farm was in the news earlier in the year when Friends of the Earth revealed that the GM crop had been planted. This was despite the fact that the company responsible for the crop, AgrEvo, had failed to advertise the planting in a local paper as required by Government regulations.

Pete Riley, Food campaigner at Friends of the Earth said:
> "The destruction of this crop is further evidence of public concern over GM crops. Friends of the Earth is not opposed in principle to scientific trials of GM crops, but we think that the current farm-scale trials and the other GM tests taking place around the UK pose an unacceptable risk to the environment and will not provide the information we need for an informed judgment on GM crops. The Government must call a five year freeze on GM food and crops. GM trials should only take place under strict controls."

Jean Saunders of Swindon Friends of the Earth said:
> "Local people will be delighted that Mr Barker has destroyed this crop – we have had unprecedented support in the town since we discovered a few weeks ago that he was growing GM crops. We believe that, in AgrEvo's rush to push ahead with this first farm-scale trial, Captain Barker was badly advised about the dangers of genetic pollution. We congratulate the trustees for taking the cautious approach and stopping this trial."

Friends of the Earth has major criticisms of the farm-scale trials of GM crops. These include: inadequate pollen barriers to protect neighbouring farmers and wildlife, failure to consult adequately on the scientific design of the trials and failure to survey wildlife before the trials started.

Contact details: Contact name: Tel number: Fax number:

Useful contacts

Part 7

1 Useful addresses

Black Environment Network
9, Llainwen Uchaf, Llanberis,
Gwynedd, LL55 4LL
Tel: 01286 870715

Charities Aid Foundation
King's Hill, West Malling, Kent, ME19 4TA
Tel: 01732 520000
Website: www.cafonline.org

Charity Commission for England and Wales
Harmsworth House, 13-15 Bouverie Street,
London, EC4Y 8DP
Tel: 0870 333 0123
E-mail: feedback@charity-commission.gov.uk
Website: www.charity-commission.gov.uk

Charter 88
16-24 Underwood Street, London, N1 7JQ
Tel: 020 7684 3888
E-mail: charter88.org.uk
Website: www.charter88.org.uk

Communities Against Toxics
PO Box 29, Ellesmere Port,
Cheshire CH66 3TX
Email:ralph@tcpublications.freeserve.co.uk

Community Matters (National Federation
of Community Organisations)
8-9 Upper Street, London, N1 0PQ
Tel: 020 7226 0189
Website: www.communitymatters.org.uk

Consumers Association
2 Marylebone Road, London, NW1 4DF
Tel: 020 7486 5544
Website: www.which.net

Community Development Foundation
60 Highbury Grove, London, N5 2AG
Tel: 020 7226 5375
E-mail: admin@cdf.org.uk
Website: www.cdf.org.uk

Corporate Watch
16b Cherwell Street, Oxford, OX4 1BG
Tel: 01865 791 391
E-mail mail@corporatewatch.org
Website: www.corporatewatch.org

Council for the Protection of Rural England
Warwick House, 25 Buckingham Palace
Road, London, SW1W 0PP
Tel: 020 7976 6433
E-mail: info@cpre.org.uk
Website: www.greenchannel.com/cpre/

Council for the Protection of Rural Wales
Ty Gwyn, 31 High Street, Welshpool,
Powys, SY21 7JP
E-mail: information@cprw.org.uk
Tel: 01938 552525

**Department of the Environment,
Transport and the Regions**
Eland House, Bressenden Place, London,
SW1E 5DU
Tel: 020 7890 3000
Website: www.detr.gov.uk

Directory of Social Change
24 Stephenson Way, London, NW1 2DP
Tel: 020 7209 1015
E-mail: info@dsc.org.uk
Website: www.dsc.org.uk

Environmental Law Foundation
Suite 309, 16 Baldwins Gardens, London,
EC1N 7RJ
Tel: 020 7404 1030
E-mail: info@elf-net.org
Website: www.greenchannel.com/elf/

Ethical Property Company
43 St Giles, Oxford, OX1 3LW
Tel: 01865 316338
E-mail: epc@centres.demon.co.uk
Website: www.centres.demon.co.uk

Friends of the Earth (England Wales and
Northern Ireland)
26 - 28 Underwood Street,
London, N1 7JQ
Tel: 020 7490 1555
E-mail: info@foe.co.uk
Website: www.foe.co.uk

Friends of the Earth Scotland
Bonnington Mill, 72 Newhaven Road,
Edinburgh, EH6 5QG
Tel: 0131 554 9977
E-mail: enquiries@foe-scotland.org.uk
Website: www.foe-scotland.org.uk

Gaming Board for Great Britain
Berkshire House, 168-173 High Holborn,
London WC1V 7AA
Tel: 020 7306 6200

House of Commons
London, SW1A 0AA
Tel: 020 7219 3000

Liberty (National Council for Civil
Liberties)
21 Tabard Street, London, SE1 4LA
Tel: 020 7403 3888
E-mail: infor@liberty-human-rights.org.uk
Website: www.liberty-human-rights.org.uk

National Assembly for Wales
Cardiff Bay, Cardiff, CF99 1NA
Tel: 029 2089 8200
E-mail: assembly.info@wales.gsi.gov.uk
Website: www.wales.gov.uk

National Association of Citizens Advice
Bureaux
Middleton House, 115-123 Pentonville
Road, London, N1 9LZ
Tel: 020 7833 2181
Website: www.nacab.org.uk

National Association of Councils for
Voluntary Service
3rd Floor, Arundel Court, 177 Arundel
Street, Sheffield, S1 2NU
Tel: 0114 278 6636
E-mail: nacvs@nacvs.org.uk
Website: www.nacvs.org.uk

National Council for Voluntary
Organisations
Regent's Wharf, 8 All Saints Street,
London, N1 9RL
Tel: 020 7713 6161
E-mail: ncvo@ncvo-vol.org.uk
Website: www.ncvo-vol.org.uk

New Economics Foundation
Cinnamon House, 6-8 Cole Street,
London SE1 4YH
Tel: 020 7407 7447
E-mail: info@neweconomics.org
Website: www.neweconomics.org

Northern Ireland Council for Voluntary
Action
127 Ormeau Road, Belfast, BT7 1SH
Tel: 02890 321224
E-mail: info@nicva.org
Website: www.nicva.org

National Lottery Charities Board (main office, but it does have regional offices)
The Corporate Office, 16 Suffolk Street., London, SW1Y 4NL
Tel: 020 7747 5299
E-mail: enquiries@nlcb.org.uk
Website: www.nlcb.org.uk

The Neighbourhood Initiatives Foundation
The Poplars, Lightmoor, Telford, Shropshire, TF4 3QN
Tel: 01952 590777
E-mail   nif@cableinet.co.uk
Website: www.nif.co.uk

Pedestrians Association
3rd Floor, 31-33 Bondway, London, SW8 1SJ
Tel:020 7820 1010
E-mail: info@pedestrians.org.uk
Website: www.pedestrians.org.uk

Planning Aid
Royal Town Planning Institute,
Unit 319, The Custard Factory, Gibb Street, Birmingham, B9 4AA
Tel: 0121 693 1201
E-mail: isilvera@planaid.rtpi.org.uk
Website:
www.rtpi.org.ukwww.ibmpcug.co.uk/~rtpi/advice/aidlist.htm

Planning Aid Scotland
Bonnington Mill, 72 Newhaven Road, Edinburgh, EH6 5QG
Tel: 0131 555 1565
E-mail: pas@sol.co.uk

Planning Aid Wales
The Maltings, East Tyndall Street, Cardiff, CF24 5EA
Tel: 029 2048 5767
Website: members.aol.com/planaid

Scottish Council for Voluntary Organisations
18-19 Claremont Crescent, Edinburgh, EH7 4QD
Tel: 0131 556 3882
E-mail: maureen.thom@scvo.org.uk
Website: www.scvo.org.uk

Sustain
94 White Lion Street,
London, N1 9PF
Tel: 020 7837 1228
E-mail: sustain@sustainweb.org
Website: www.sustainweb.org

Transport 2000
The Impact Centre, 12-18 Hoxton Street, London N1 6NG
Tel: 020 7613 0743
E-mail:
transport2000@transport2000.demon.co.uk

UK Communities Online
www.communities.org.uk
Overall aim is to encourage individuals to share experience and practice and to join in their own local online community.

Wales Council for Voluntary Action
Llys Ifor, Crescent Road, Caerphilly, CF83 1XL
Tel: 029 2085 5100
E-mail: enquiries@wcva.org.uk
Website: www.wcva.org.uk

2 Useful reading

General

How to win – fact sheets
Friends of the Earth is compiling a set of 10 fact sheets on the following aspects of local campaigning:
1 The law
2 The planning system
3 Access to information
4 Changes in local government
5 The corporate sector
6 Europe
7 Northern Ireland
8 Wales
9 Regionalisation
10 Scotland

For more information about getting hold of these, please contact Friends of the Earth Publications, 56-58 Alma Street, Luton LU1 2PH or Tel: 020 7490 1555.

Free Department of the Environment, Transport and the Regions leaflets and publicity material are available from: DETR Free Literature, PO Box 236, Wetherby, West Yorkshire, LS23 7NB, Tel: 0870 1226236

Campaign guides

The Campaigning Handbook
Mark Lattimer 2nd edition
A comprehensive guide to planning your campaign, direct action, lobbying and the law. Published by The Directory of Social Change. £15.95

Protecting Our Environment (2nd Edition)
Available from: Friends Of The Earth Scotland, Bonnington Mill, 72 Newhaven Road, Edinburgh EH6 5QP, Tel: 0131 554 8656
A citizen's guide to environmental rights and action, £4.95.

Community campaigning

Community Groups Handbook (2nd Edition) £6.95
Available from: Community Development Foundation, CDF Publications, 60 Highbury Grove, London N5 2AG
This handbook draws on interviews with community activists and describes tried and tested methods for taking action.
Environment Action Pack: Practical Ideas for Community Organisations
Available from: Community Development Foundation, CDF Publications, 60 Highbury Grove, London N5 2AG
£6.00.

Countryside and biodiversity campaign handbooks

Campaigners' Guide to Trees & Woods
Available from: CPRE, Warwick House, 25 Buckingham Palace Road, London SW1W 0PP, Tel: 020 7976 6433
A guide for anyone wanting to influence tree and woodland planting, woodland protection, management and planning, £10.

Saving Wildlife Sites
Available from: Friends of the Earth Publications, 56-58 Alma Street, Luton LU1 2PH, Tel: 020 7490 1555
A manual for local campaigners, covering all aspects of campaigning to save and protect wildlife sites, £4.50.

Fundraising guides

Fundraising and Events
Organising Local Events
Tried and Tested Ideas for Raising Money Locally
All three titles by Sarah Passingham
Available from Directory of Social Change Publications. Each costs £9.95.

Writing better Fundraising Applications
Michael Norton and Mike Eastwood
Published by the Directory of Social
Change. Excellent ideas to help you
produce effective funding applications,
£12.95.

The Directory of Social Change also
produces regional guides to local trusts.
These should be available in your local
library. They are updated every
two years.

Legal
Encyclopaedia of Environmental Law
Encyclopaedia of Planning Law and
  Practice
Both titles published by Sweet and
Maxwell. These encyclopaedias are key
references, available at University Law
libraries or good public libraries.

Media contacts
Writers and Artists Yearbook
Published by A & C Black
Annual update of information about local
and regional print and broadcast media,
£11.99.

Mineral campaigns
Campaigners' Guide to Minerals
Available from: CPRE, Warwick House, 25
Buckingham Palace Road, London
SW1W OPP, Tel: 020 7976 6433, £10.

Campaigners' Guide to Opencast Coal
Mining
Available from: CPRE, Warwick House, 25
Buckingham Palace Road, London
SW1W OPP, Tel: 020 7976 6433, £10.

Northern Ireland – key guides for campaigners
Northern Ireland Environmental Law
S Turner and K Morrow
Published by Gill and MacMillan.

Northern Ireland Planning System – a
user's guide
Available from: Friends of the Earth
Northern Ireland, 40 Wellington
Park, Belfast BT9 6DN, Tel: 028 90 664311,
£3.

Planning & development
Campaigners' Guide to Local Plans
Available from: CPRE, Warwick House, 25
Buckingham Palace Road, London
SW1W OPP, Tel: 020 7976 6433, £10 or
try the free summary available with SAE.
Campaigners' Guide to Public Inquiries &
Planning Appeals
Available from: CPRE, Warwick House, 25
Buckingham Palace Road, London
SW1W OPP, Tel: 020 7976 6433, £10.

Community Planning and Building
Available from Planning Aid Publications,
Calvert House, 5 Calvert Avenue, London
E2 7JP
A guide to how individuals and
community groups can improve their
environment, £5.95 + 50p p&p.

How to Campaign Against Supermarket
Developments
Available from: Sustain, 94 White Lion
Street, London N1 9PF Tel: 020
7837 1228, £3.

How to Stop and Influence Planning
Permission
Speer and Dade
Published by Stonepound Books, Tel:
01273 842155, £12.50.

Responding to Planning Applications
Available from: CPRE, Warwick House, 25
Buckingham Palace Road, London
SW1W OPP, Tel: 020 7976 6433
A useful guide showing how to get
involved with planning decisions to
protect your local environment, free.

Stopping the Sprawl
Available from: Friends of the Earth
Publications, 56-58 Alma Street, Luton
LU1 2PH, Tel: 020 7490 1555
This guide explains how individuals can
campaign to change housing plans at a
local level, £7.

Pollution campaigns
The Polluting Factory Campaign Guide
Available from: Friends of the Earth
Publications, 56-58 Alma Street, Luton
LU1 2PH, Tel: 020 7490 1555, £15.
The Incineration Campaign Guide
Available from: Friends of the Earth
Publications, 56-58 Alma Street, Luton
LU1 2PH, Tel: 020 7490 1555, £15.

The Landfill Campaign Guide
Available from: Friends of the Earth
Publications, 56-58 Alma Street, Luton
LU1 2PH, Tel: 020 7490 1555, £15.

Transport campaigns
Fighting Road Schemes
Available from: Friends of the Earth
Publications, 56-58 Alma Street, Luton
LU1 2PH, Tel: 020 7490 1555, £4.50.

Living Streets
Available from: Transport 2000, The
Impact Centre, 12-18 Hoxton Street,
London N1 6NG, Tel: 020 7613 0743
A guide to cutting traffic and reclaiming
street space, £10.

Our Kind of Town
Available from: The Pedestrian
Association, Third Floor, 31-33 Bondway
London SW8 1SJ
A guide on how to improve town centres,
£5.

Taming the Traffic
Available from: Friends of the Earth
Publications, 56-58 Alma Street, Luton
LU1 2PH, Tel: 020 7490 1555, £10.

The Walking Bus
Available from: Friends of the Earth
Publications, 56-58 Alma Street, Luton
LU1 2PH, Tel: 020 7490 1555.

The Walking Class
Available from: The Pedestrian
Association, Third Floor, 31-33 Bondway
London SW8 1SJ.
How to develop green travel to school,
including case studies, £8

Walkways Advice Pack
Our Kind of Town
Available from: The Pedestrian
Association, Third Floor, 31-33 Bondway
London SW8 1SJ
How to campaign for safe crossings and
traffic calming, £5.

Web and HTML tips
HTML: the Definitive Guide
(ISBN: 1565924924), £23.40

HTML 4 for the World Wide Web
4th edition Visual QuickStart Guide
(ISBN: 0201354934)
Published by Peachpit Press, £14.99.

Online tutorials:
http://www.gettingstarted.net/
http://hotwired.lycos.com/webmonkey/auth
oring/html_basics/

Support Friends of the Earth

Better environment, better life

Friends of the Earth works to protect and improve the conditions for life on Earth, now and for the future. We believe that looking after the planet is the best way of looking after people. Join us today and help create a safer, healthier, fairer world.

Contact us on **020 7490 1555** for more information on how to:

- ⊙ Make donations by personal cheque, credit card or charity voucher.
- ⊙ Make regular donations by standing order, which provides secure funding for our campaigns.
- ⊙ Join Campaign Express and receive free, regular action packs that show you how you can take small, simple actions that have a big impact.
- ⊙ Join your nearest local group – call 0990 224488 or visit our website.
- ⊙ Buy publications, like this, from our extensive catalogue.

FRIENDS *of the*
earth
for the planet for people